Circular Walks in Wirral

Field path near Brimstage

Circular walks in *Wirral*

Seventeen circular walks
exploring Wirral's finest countryside

Carl Rogers

MARA BOOKS

www.marabooks.co.uk
www.northerneyebooks.co.uk

First published in April 1995 by Mara Books, 22 Crosland Terrace, Helsby, Frodsham, Cheshire, WA6 9LY.

Second edition published May 1999

Third edition published November 2004

Fourth edition published April 2012

Fifth edition published 2017

ISBN 978-1-902512-21-1

Illustration on page 62 by Roger Oldham, taken from *'Picturesque Cheshire'* by T.A. Coward.

British Library Cataloguing-in-publication data.
A catalogue for this book is available from the British Library.

Whilst every effort has been made to ensure that the information contained in this book is correct, the author or the publisher can accept no responsibility for errors, loss or injury, however caused.

Maps based on out of copyright Ordnance Survey mapping.

Contents

A map of Wirral and location of the walks

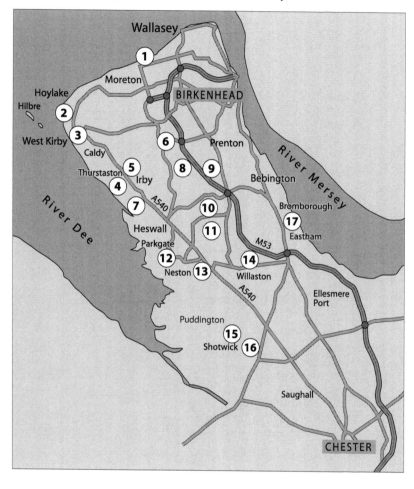

Introduction

MANY ASSOCIATE Wirral with industry and urban sprawl, but look a little further and you will find that much of the rural charm and character that once made Wirral famous has survived the relentless development of the last hundred years or so. Even those living in the very centre of towns such as Birkenhead, Wallasey or Bebbington are rarely more than a few miles from open country which, in detail, is every bit as attractive today as it was a century ago.

Surely the finest (and cheapest) way to enjoy this countryside is on foot, and Wirral has one of the most frequently used and best maintained footpath networks in the country. These paths will take you through the best of Wirral's varied and historic landscape. Here you can enjoy quiet field paths or extensive views from the sandstone ridge; walk across miles of tidal sands or watch seals from a windswept island with a recorded history reaching back over 1,200 years. Perhaps quiet woodlands are more your scene or bird watching on the vast salt marshes at Neston or Parkgate. All this is available within the tiny area which we know today as Wirral.

Walking on the beach at West Kirby

A brief history

ALTHOUGH Wirral's history reaches way back into prehistoric times, its greatest influence and the one which is responsible for the appearance of Wirral today, has been the development of the two adjacent cities of Chester and Liverpool. It was the use of Chester and the River Dee by the Romans that gives us our first glimpse of Wirral almost 2,000 years ago and influenced its development for the next 1,700 years. The decline of Chester as a port—caused by the loss of the River Dee's navigable water—along with the rapid growth of Liverpool, has resulted in the modern settlement pattern that we see today.

Before the Romans, Wirral would have been inhabited by numerous tribes associated with the Neolithic, Bronze Age and Iron Age cultures common to the rest of England and Wales. Unfortunately there are very few remains of their passing in Wirral, despite the fact that a coastal location such as this would have been very attractive to prehistoric settlers with its gentle terrain and sheltered location.

When the Romans arrived, Wirral was inhabited by members of the Celtic tribe known as the Cornovii, who occupied most of Cheshire and Shropshire. They had their capital at Wroxeter near Shrewsbury and were generally peaceful and easily subdued by the Romans. They did build hill forts, although none are known to exist in Wirral—the nearest being the two small enclosures which crown the summits of Helsby Hill and Woodhouse Hill to the south.

The arrival of the Romans at Chester would have had a great impact on Wirral. Chester (Deva) was the main fortresses in this part of Britain and a network of roads connected it to the rest of the country. Wirral's fertile land would no doubt have been brought into cultivation and used to feed the soldiers of the Twentieth Legion stationed there. It was the Romans who first brought the River Dee into use as a commercial seaway (although trading ships are known to have been regular visitors to western Britain centuries before this) which continued for the next 1,500 years.

Two thousand years ago the River Dee was very different to the vast expanse of tidal sands, marsh and reclaimed farmland that we see today. Much of the original coastline is now many miles inland and over one third of the original estuary has been reclaimed. Despite this, the old coastline can still be traced following a line southeast from Parkgate past Little Neston to Burton

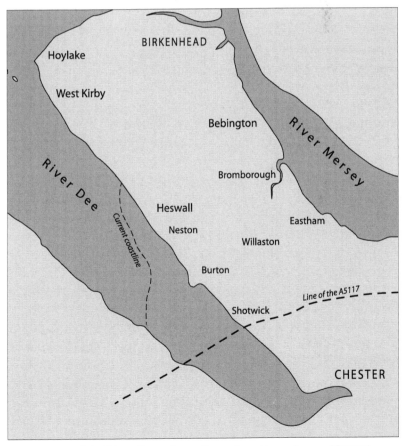

A map of the River Dee prior to the reclamation schemes (C1700)

Point—originally a rocky headland jutting into the estuary. From there the coastline continued to Shotwick, where the ancient church stands less than a stone's throw from the old river bank, and on to the site of Shotwick Castle, once a small port used as the embarkation point for troops travelling to Ireland (see walk 16). South of the castle, the river bank becomes higher and culminates in Blacon Point, an exposed headland which originally overlooked the river. This is now topped by the housing estates and high rise tower blocks of Blacon. The flat land between Blacon Point and Chester—currently occupied by the retail developments around Sealand Road—was originally a large shallow bay, while the port itself lay close to the city walls near the Roodee.

The existence of the port at Chester would have brought ships from all over the Roman Empire and their square rigged galleys must have been a common site from the headlands at Burton and Blacon. To protect this approach to the port, the Romans are thought to have established an outpost near Meols at the northwestern tip of Wirral, along with a road which linked it to the fort at Chester.

When the Romans left Britain the east coast was quickly colonised by Saxons from the Continent and the expanding kingdoms they established began to reach western Britain by the second half of the sixth century. A great victory by the Saxons of Northumbria against the Celts at the Battle of Chester in AD 616 marked the beginning of the displacement of the British tribes in Cheshire. From a study of place names we know that Cheshire came under Saxon control very quickly and the British (who from this time came to be known as the 'Welsh') were pushed west beyond the Dee into Wales.

While this seems to have been the case in most of Cheshire, Wirral appears to have been slightly different. A handful of Welsh place names have survived indicating that the Celtic influence remained in Wirral longer than elsewhere. Landican and Liscard are the most obvious examples and contain the common Welsh place name elements of *'llan'* a church foundation and *'llys'* meaning court or hall. Both these place name elements are common throughout Wales today. The Saxon advance into Cheshire evidently pushed the Celts into this northern part of Wirral which, unlike today, would have been a remote part of the peninsula being farthest away from the city of Chester.

Another indication, and one which suggests an even later Celtic presence in Wirral is the name Wallasey, from the Norse 'Walla's—ey' meaning 'Welshman's island'. Wirral was settled by Norsemen from Ireland during the late tenth and early eleventh centuries and their name for this corner of Wirral no doubt records their impression of its inhabitants. Until recent times it was separated from the rest of Wirral by the inlet of Wallasey Pool and only connected by a thin strip of shifting sands along the north coast; it would thus have made a logical retreat for the remaining Celts in Wirral. It may even have been a true island at that time as a study of the bedrock and coastal deposits around Wallasey confirm that at some time in the past it was completely separated from the rest of Wirral.

The earthwork remains of Shotwick Castle

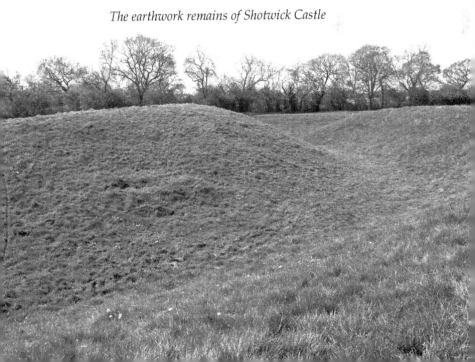

The Vikings harassed the entire western seaboard of Britain and were well known for their ruthless and brutal attacks. These were often followed by colonisation and several of their settlement names have survived in Wirral. They can be identified today by the ending *'by'* and *'wall'*, whilst settlements of Saxon origin use *'ton'* and *'ham'*. The Norse settlements remained close to the sea and they are concentrated today in the northwestern parts of Wirral. The fact that Wirral was an important centre to the Norse who settled here is verified by the existence of the name Thingwall. The *'thing'* element of this name identifies it as the site of a local parliament and is similar in origin to Dingwall in Scotland and Tynwald in the Isle of Man.

When the Normans came to Britain they formed no new settlements, they simply took control of the existing civil structure. The nearby city of Chester is thought to have passed through a period of decay after the Romans, but by the time of the Norman Conquest it was a thriving city again. Like the Saxons before them, the Normans found it difficult to extend their influence much beyond the Welsh border and Chester was ideally placed to launch attacks into the kingdom of Gwynedd which proved to be the most troublesome of the independent Welsh kingdoms.

William the Conqueror established powerful barons in key positions along what is still the Welsh border today and gave them almost unlimited power in an attempt to bring the Welsh under Norman rule. They were encouraged to attack and plunder their Welsh neighbours in order to extend their own power and influence. At Chester he installed his nephew Hugh de Avranches, otherwise known as 'Hugh Lupus'. For the next few centuries Wirral became part of the troubled border country

The castle at Shotwick is thought to have been built by the Normans about this time to guard a ford across the River Dee into Wales and as a base to launch attacks into Wales and Ireland. Henry II and Henry III, along with Edward I are all thought to have used the castle in their campaigns against the Welsh and

Irish. After Edward's victory against Llywelyn in 1283 the castle had no further use and was allowed to become a ruin.

During the Middle Ages, Chester reached its zenith as an international trading centre, but by then its days as a port were numbered. The river began to silt up and large ships were no longer able to reach the city. To remedy this, an anchorage was established at Shotwick where there were already facilities near the old castle. An anchorage behind the sheltering arm of Burton Point was also used for a while, but the merchants of Chester realised that if they were to hold onto their trade, something more substantial had to be done. This took the form of the port known as the 'New Key', begun in 1541 at Little Neston where deep water could still be found. Remains of the old sandstone quayside and customs house can still be seen on the marsh edge (walks 12 and 13). There were major problems in the funding and building of this quay and it was never a success.

By the turn of the century the search was on for a new port as the river continued to silt up. A new anchorage was tried at Parkgate and for a time it became one of the main embarkation

The Water Tower, Chester, built to defend
the approach to the old port

The 'New Cut' built around 1725

points for Ireland, with many famous individuals making the crossing from here. By the turn of the nineteenth century however, the water was too shallow for boats to dock and the River Dee as a commercial waterway finally died.

Ironically, it was one of the attempts made to improve the navigability of the river which accelerated siltation along the Wirral coast. About 1725 the River Dee was confined to a canal which ran from Saltney to Connah's Quay. This took the low water channel over to the Welsh side of the estuary and although for the remainder of its journey it was left to follow its former course, a gradual move to the west had begun. Since then the low water channel—where the deepest water is to be found—has moved gradually away from the Wirral coast, and sands, followed by mud and marsh grass, have replaced it.

This 'New Cut', as it was called, also caused the loss of a deep water anchorage at the mouth of the estuary known as 'High Lake' or 'Hyle Lake'. This had been used for centuries as a safe, sheltered anchorage, being protected by a long sand bar that reached right across the mouth of the river. It was from here that the forces of William of Orange sailed to defeat James II at the Battle of the Boyne in 1689. It had also been frequented by ships waiting to approach a tiny insignificant fishing settlement near the mouth of the Mersey known as Liverpool.

As the last commercial ship was leaving the River Dee, Liverpool was growing fast and soon became the main port in northwest England. One of its more infamous activities was its involvement in the slave trade with Africa and the plantations of the West Indies.

The beach at Parkgate around 1910

Throughout the second half of the eighteenth century Liverpool expanded rapidly and its ships were trading throughout the world. On the Wirral side of the river lay the isolated headlands of Wallasey and Birkenhead, previously quiet backwaters situated away from the commercial centre of Chester and the Deeside ports. Now things were very different.

We have already mentioned the 'Welshman's island' and its isolation beyond the water of Wallasey Pool. On the south side of the Pool was a headland known as Birkenhead, bounded to the south by the tidal inlet of Tranmere Pool. It was here on the 'headland of the birches' in 1150 that a Benedictine Abbey had been founded, the ruins of which still stand amongst the urban sprawl of the modern town. As always, the abbey site had been well chosen and occupied a quiet, beautiful location away from the 'corruption' of the city where the monks could live their 'contemplative life' in the 'worship of God'. The monks enjoyed many privileges including fishing and the rights of ferryage. These were to be snatched away from them and their land confiscated with Henry VIII's Dissolution of the Monasteries in 1536.

Birkenhead remained quiet, peaceful and little more than a hamlet until the turn of the nineteenth century when, in 1810 its population numbered just 109. This could also be said of Wallasey, Liscard and Seacombe—tiny rural settlements at this time. With the rise of Liverpool however, such nearby beauty had the wealthy merchants of Liverpool looking across the river for sites for their new homes. Steam ferryboats were introduced in 1820 and a regular, daily service could now be guaranteed. The grand houses of Hamilton Square were the result. Within ten years the population of Birkenhead had grown to 2,569 and by 1841 it numbered over 8,000.

The commercial possibilities of Wallasey Pool were hard to ignore and by 1844 work on Wallasey docks was started. The land around the river inlet was reclaimed and the natural beauty of Wallasey Pool was gone for ever. The docks thrived for a while and became famous the world over for the shipbuilding of Cammell Laird's.

Unfortunately Birkenhead grew too rapidly and without proper controls; as a result the fine start at Hamilton Square and the nearby Park were not continued. Today Birkenhead, Seacombe, Liscard and Wallasey have become suburbs of Liverpool and almost all their natural features have been smothered by bricks, concrete and tarmac.

Hamilton Square

North Wirral Coastal Park

Distance: *6½ miles/10km*

This walk offers a mixture of urban seafront and sand dunes. There are wide views across Liverpool Bay to North Wales and east along the north Wirral coast to Liverpool.

Start: Begin the walk in Meols at the northern end of 'Meols Parade'. There is parking available on the seafront along with public toilets.
Grid ref: 233 906. (Landranger 108, Explorer 266)

The walk

1. This is the southern end of the North Wirral Coastal Park and the beginning of the great concrete embankment which stretches all the way to New Brighton. Take the path which follows the top of the embankment and allows you a view both out to sea and inland. If you walk along the concrete road partway down the embankment itself your view is much more restricted.

After about a mile you pass the prominent landmark of Leasowe Lighthouse which has been visible since the start of the walk. In the opposite direction, when the tide is out, sands stretch almost as far as the eye can see, but when the water returns the strength of this embankment becomes crucial to the nearby towns of Moreton and Leasowe. Prior to its building in the nineteenth century, the sea frequently flooded inland over much of the flat land now occupied by Leasowe, Moreton, Meols and Hoylake. This is one of the reasons why the north coast was so sparsely populated in the past, with the result that few really old buildings will be seen in these areas today.

One exception is the next prominent landmark which lies about another mile along the coast—Leasowe Castle. Now much added to, the original structure was built in 1593 by Fernando, the fifth Earl of Derby for viewing the race meetings which were a frequent event on the

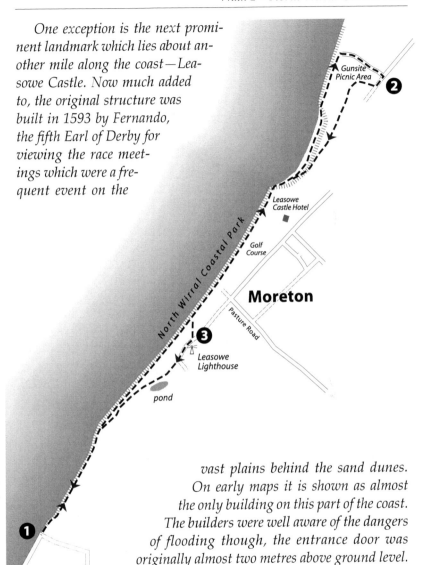

vast plains behind the sand dunes. On early maps it is shown as almost the only building on this part of the coast. The builders were well aware of the dangers of flooding though, the entrance door was originally almost two metres above ground level.

After the Civil War, the castle came into the possession of the Edgertons of Oulton and it entered a period of decay. The sorry state of the building at this time earned it the name 'Mockbeggar Hall', which appears on the maps of Collins 1687 and Burdett 1777.

Leasowe Castle

Beyond Leasowe Castle the embankment curves into a small bay and the path takes you almost onto the sand. Continue on the path immediately above the beach to the next car park. Walk through the car park and follow the road where it turns right. Shortly there are two parking areas on the right (the car parks and the picnic areas are known as the 'Gunsite Picnic Area').

This name recalls the anti-aircraft guns which were stationed here during World War II to protect nearby Liverpool from German air raids.

2. Turn right into the second car park. Take the path in the bottom right-hand corner and walk straight ahead across the open grass to a kissing gate which leads onto a path through the sand dunes. At a T junction in about 30m turn left, then turn left again up steps in about 20m. A good path now runs along the top of the sand dunes for almost ½ mile.

Where the path joins the embankment, turn left and retrace the outward journey until you are level with Leasowe Lighthouse. Turn left here and walk across the grass to the lighthouse.

This imposing structure rises to a height of 101 feet and can be seen from almost anywhere on the north coast. A date of 1763 can be seen above the doorway, but this is said to have been taken from an earlier light; the present structure dating from 1824. It was last used in 1908 and has narrowly escaped demolition over the years. It is now open to the public on the first Sunday of the month.

3. With your back to the lighthouse, turn left along the road and just after the car park, take the right fork. Follow this track past a pool on the left and continue to eventually reach the well-used path which backs the embankment. Turn left and return to the car park in Meols to complete the walk.

This western end of the embankment is the approximate site of Wirral's celebrated 'Submerged Forest'. The forest has now disappeared, its last remains buried by sand over 50 years ago, although traces do appear occasionally. Many of Wirral's notable writers make mention of it and it was noted by William Webb as early as 1622.

The sumerged forest, Meols

In his book 'The Wirral Peninsula', *the late Norman Ellison describes the forest as it appeared during the 1930s in this way: 'The clean stretch of sand was broken by a black patch, perhaps a half-mile in length, which a closer inspection revealed to be a thick stratum of peat, brown twigs, leaves, mosses, ferns and lichens, all tightly compressed. Above this mass, a large number of tree trunks, perhaps three or four feet high, stood erect, whilst many fallen trunks and large branches lay partly buried.'*

This bizarre 'forest' seems to have been the result of inundation by the sea into an area of ancient woodland before the clearances of the Middle Ages—possibly the erosion or collapse of sheltering sand dunes which have now completely disappeared. The coastline is an area of constant change and the area of north Wirral is known to have undergone considerable change in fairly recent times.

One of the hardest puzzles to solve regarding the forest is not its existence, but the vast quantity of antiquities which have been discovered there. In all over 5,000 objects have been recorded with an interval of around 1,700 years between the earliest and latest finds. These include Saxon, Greek and Roman coins, spurs, daggers, swords, keys, buckles, brooches, harnesses and many other items too numerous to mention. Even with the existence of the anchorage at nearby Hoyle Lake and the Roman outpost which is thought to have existed at Meols, it is still difficult to explain how such vast quantities of objects with such a large time span came to be gathered together in so small an area.

Caldy & Hoylake

Distance: *8½ miles/13.5km*

An exploration of Wirral's northwestern tip—from the tidal sands of the River Dee to the quiet woodlands of Stapledon and the wide views from Grange Hill above West Kirby.

Start: Parking is available in a sizable car park at the Wirral Country Park in 'Croft Drive', 'Caldy Road', Caldy. *Grid ref: 223 850 (Landranger 108, Explorer 266).*

The walk

1. From the car park head north (right-wards) along the Wirral Way (towards West Kirby). In about 300m, take a path (kissing gate) on the left which leads to a viewpoint overlooking the tidal sands of the River Dee.

This gives a grand view across the River Dee to the hills of Flintshire and Denbighshire and also along the North Wales coast to the rocky headland of the Great Orme and the northern spurs of the Carneddau mountains in Snowdonia.

Continue along the grassy cliff-top to either join a road end ('Macdona Drive') near bungalows on the outskirts of West Kirby or drop down onto the sand if the tide allows. For the latter option walk along the beach to the southern end of the Marine Lake. If the tide is too high to walk along the sand, reach the Marine Lake by following 'Macdona Drive' and turning left into 'Sandy Lane'.

Follow the tarmac footpath along the outside edge of the Marine Lake unless the tide is very high. If this is the case turn right and walk along 'South Parade' with the Marine Lake to

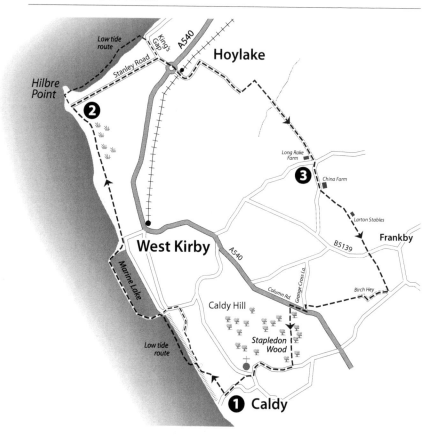

your left. At the northern end of the lake, immediately after the sailing club, drop down onto the sand and walk ahead (north) along the beach and salt marsh to Hilbre Point.

The sand dunes to the right are a reminder of how wild and wind-swept this northwestern tip of Wirral was until quite recently. Before the modern developments and sea defences around Meols and Hoylake were built, the entire north coast was composed of shifting sand dunes and marshes which were constantly changing and being inundated by the sea.

The dune system and adjacent reed beds are managed by the Cheshire Wildlife Trust as a nature reserve (Red Rocks Nature Reserve, which is owned by the Royal Liverpool Golf Club). The area is a haven for wildlife and is notable for being one of the breeding grounds for the rare natterjack toad.

2. At Hilbre Point turn right and walk along 'Stanley Road' to its junction with 'The Kings Gap' (crossroads) by the 'Green Lodge Hotel'. Turn right here and at a roundabout in the centre of Hoylake go straight ahead into 'Station Road'.

(As an alternative to this if the tide allows, you can follow the shore between Hilbre Point and 'North Parade', the road which runs along the seafront in Hoylake. At 'North Parade', turn right into 'The King's Gap' and walk straight ahead to the roundabout.)

Hoylake has changed dramatically in the last 150 years. It originated as a tiny fishing village and took its name from the deep water pool used by ships for centuries as a safe anchorage in their approach to the ports of Chester and later Liverpool. Known 'High Lake' or 'Hoyle Lake'. It was protected from the often stormy waters of the Irish Sea by a massive sand bar known as 'Hoyle Sand', covered only by the highest spring tides. Behind this sheltering arm the lake retained 5 to 10 metres of water at low tide and was reported to have been over half a mile wide.

One of the most important events to happen here was the embarkation of William III's army to engage the forces of James II at the Battle of the Boyne in 1689. Over 23 regiments were sent under the Duke of Schomberg to Chester and then to ships waiting in Hoyle Lake. There are said to have been over 90 vessels anchored here in expectation of William's army. The road which leads down to North Parade is now known as 'The King's Gap' and no doubt recalls this event.

Hoyle Lake remained one of the embarkation points for Ireland throughout the seventeenth century. Those hoping to make the journey waited at Chester until a ship was available. They then came here where they often had to wait days for favourable weather conditions. Despite this, there are said to have been only two houses at Hoylake.

The confining of the River Dee to the 'New Cut' around 1725 resulted in the sand bar of Hoyle Sand being cut in two. This led to the silting up of the pool and today there is no trace of it.

By the end of the eighteenth century the new-found pastime of sea bathing was gathering popularity and the sands building up along the north coast created a fine beach at Hoylake. Sir John Stanley, who owned much of the land in the vicinity, built the Royal Hotel in 1794 and began Hoylake's development as a seaside resort which continued until the mid-twentieth century.

After a level crossing, continue ahead along 'Carr Lane', through an industrial estate and eventually past houses. At the end of the lane ('Yeoman Cottages' on the right), an unsurfaced farm track continues ahead into fields (Footpath 19). At the end of the concrete fence posts on the left, continue straight ahead for about 120m to a junction of paths (fingerpost). Turn left here and look for a signed path and stile on the right after about 270m (shortly after a junction of overhead power cables). Turn right here and follow the path along the field edge to a wooden farm bridge over the River Birket. The path now broadens into a farm track which continues straight ahead to join 'Saughall Massie Road' near 'Long Rake Farm'.

3. Cross the road and walk along the curiously named 'China Farm Lane' (opposite). Immediately after 'China Farm', bear left into fields onto the signed 'Public footpath to Frankby'. Walk diagonally across the field to a stile and fingerpost in the right-hand corner. Cross the stile and keep to the right-hand field edge. Turn right over a stile and small footbridge and bear left immediately to walk parallel to the stream for about 25m. At a rough driveway turn right. This eventually leads onto the access road to 'Larton Stables' on the left. Follow the access road to 'Frankby Road' (B5139).

Cross over and continue on the well-used path directly opposite (signed to 'Thurstaston'). At the end of the path turn sharp right and walk along an access road ('Birch Hey'). At the end of the track an old stone stile takes you into fields with a fine view ahead to Caldy Hill and Stapledon Woods backed by the Welsh hills.

Keep beside the hedge and at the bottom of the field cross the stile and footbridge which lead into an enclosed footpath between gardens. At 'Grange Cross Lane' turn left, then right at 'Column Road'. After about 200m cross over and look for the signed path up stone steps into Stapledon Wood on the left (FP 48). Follow the path straight ahead parallel to the edge of the wood on the left ignoring a path on the right. At the far side of the wood a gap in the wall leads via stone steps and a short enclosed path to 'Caldy Road' where you should turn right. Follow the road into Caldy village.

Where the road bends to the right near a stone memorial in front of the church and about 30m after 'Croft Drive', bear left onto a signed bridleway. The bridleway follows a driveway at first ('The Croft'), then becomes a narrow sandy path between large wooded gardens. Follow the path to the road ('Croft Drive'), turn right and return to the car park at the Wirral Way to complete the walk.

Looking to the Hilbre Islands from Hilbre Point

Caldy &
West Kirby

Distance: *3¾ miles/5km*

A walk through Caldy Woods and along the Wirral Way, with good views from The Column and Grange Hill. Footpaths are excellent throughout.

Start: Parking is available in a sizable car park at the Wirral Country Park in 'Croft Drive', Caldy.
Grid ref: 223 850 (Landranger 108, Explorer 266).

The walk

1. Walk back to the road ('Croft Drive') and turn left. In about 200m, where the road bends right, bear left onto a signed bridleway. Follow the sandy path between large wooded gardens to Caldy Road in the centre of Caldy opposite the church. Turn right and walk through the village.

This attractive village, first mentioned in the Domesday Book as 'Calders', owes its appearance to R.W. Barton, a Manchester man who bought the township in 1832. His building and renovation projects have left us with an attractive mix of red sandstone and black and white timbering.

One of these fine buildings was originally an inn owned by an enterprising landlord who is said to have made most of his money by rolling barrels of beer down the hill and selling it to workers on the West Kirby to Hooton line (now the Wirral Way) built in 1884, on pay day!

2. At the end of the high stone wall on the right, cross the road and take the signed bridleway on the left which leads into Caldy Woods (beside 'Caldecott Cottage'). Follow the path to a road and turn left. After about 200m turn right into a cul-de-sac ('Thorsway') . In about 150m, cross over and take the enclosed footpath (footpath No. 50) between gardens on the left. Turn right in the woods and bear right at the first junction to enter an open heather clearing with seats and views across to Hilbre Island and North Wales. Keep straight ahead now on the obvious path in the direction of two prominent masts ahead. Continue ahead ignoring paths on either side to the column at 'Column Road'.

This well known Wirral landmark was erected in 1841 by the Trustees of Liverpool Docks as a beacon for river traffic and replaced a large windmill used for the same purpose, destroyed by gales two years previously.

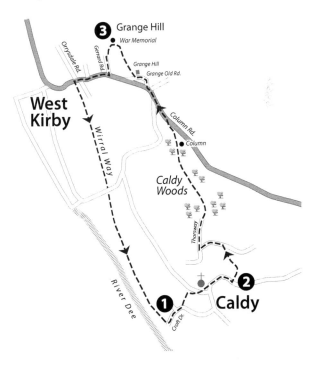

Turn left into 'Column Road' and after about 200m cross over and continue along 'Grange Old Road' (beside 'Black House Hill'). Ignore the first signed foopath on the right as the road bends and look for a well hidden footpath immediately adjacent to the drive to 'Grange Hill' (large house on the right). This path is tightly enclosed at first as it passes around the garden and above the road on the left, then leads to the war memorial on the hill itself.

'Grange Hill' was the birth place in 1830, of Charles Dawson Brown a well known local historian. Throughout his life, Brown collected all manner of antiquities which, following his death in 1890, were gathered into the Old Schoolhouse beside St. Bridgett's church in West Kirby. This was known as the 'Charles Dawson Brown Museum' and was opened in 1892. In addition, Brown wrote numerous essays which give a valuable glimpse of life in nineteenth century rural Wirral.

Caldy village

From this fine view point there is an extensive panorama. To the west, beyond the River Dee, rise the hills of North Wales, with Snowdonia and the Great Orme on the farthest horizon. Below and to the east, the green fields of north Wirral quickly give way to the reds and browns of suburbia, while the familiar Liverpool skyline peeps over the hill at Wallasey. A recent addition to this view are the off-shore wind farms which now line the northwestern horizon.

3. From the memorial, head west (left when looking out to sea and in the direction of Hilbre Island) and descend steeply beside a garden fence. At the bottom of the slope turn left along a footpath with a sandstone wall to the right to join a cul-de-sac, 'Gerrard Road'. Walk along the road and turn right down the hill. Where the road levels turn left onto the Wirral Way (opposite 'Orrysdale Road'). Follow the Wirral Way back to 'Croft Drive' car park to complete the walk (about 1½ miles).

West Kirby was originally a Norse settlement; the name means 'church town or village' (from 'Kirk'-church and 'by'-village). It was most likely established in the tenth century by Norse settlers who came by sea from Northern Ireland and settled all along the coast of northwest England. Several Norse settlements can be identified here in Wirral, usually ending with the suffix 'by'. It seems likely that it was they who built the first church here, dedicated to St. Bridgett the Irish Saint, indicating that they had become Christians by that time. In addition, several wheel headed crosses, thought to be the work of Christian Vikings, have been found at West Kirby and nearby Hilbre.

Thurstaston Common

Distance: *6½/10km or 3½ miles/5.5km*

A popular walk along Wirral's remaining undeveloped section of coastline which is still visited by each tide. Good paths then take you up on to Thurstaston Hill with its wide views across the River Dee to North Wales and over northern Wirral to Merseyside.

Start: There is plenty of parking space at the Wirral Country Park, in 'Station Road', Thurstaston. Begin the walk at the Visitor Centre. *Grid ref: 239 834 (Landranger 108, Explorer 266).*

The walk

1. From the Visitor Centre walk across the grass to the crumbling clay cliffs overlooking the beach. Turn left and follow the clifftop path to the little wooded valley of Tinker's Dell, where the path leads down wooden steps to the beach. Turn left and walk along the sand (may not be possible at certain points of the tide).

These crumbling boulder clay cliffs contain many rocks that can be traced to different parts of the country and are known as 'glacial erratics', thought to have been carried here by ancient ice sheets. The most obvious examples are the large granite boulders from Cumbria and southern Scotland which can be seen all along the cliffs.

After the cliffs become much lower and overgrown with scrub, a small stream flows onto the beach. Turn left up the path immediately before the stream. Follow the main path ahead ignoring a left fork into 'Heswall Fields', a field of National Trust land to the left. Ignore a crossing path continuing ahead between fields to a eventually reach a T junction.

North Wirral Coastal Park and Leasowe Lighthouse (walk 1)

Following Wallasey Embankment (walk 1)

Walking along the beach between West Kirby and Hilbre Point (walk 2)

Looking out to the Hilbre islands from Hilbre Point (walk 2)

Wide views can be enjoyed from Thurstaston Common (walks 4 & 5)

Shore Cottage on the beach near Thurstaston (walk 4)

Gentle field paths near Brimstage (walk 10)

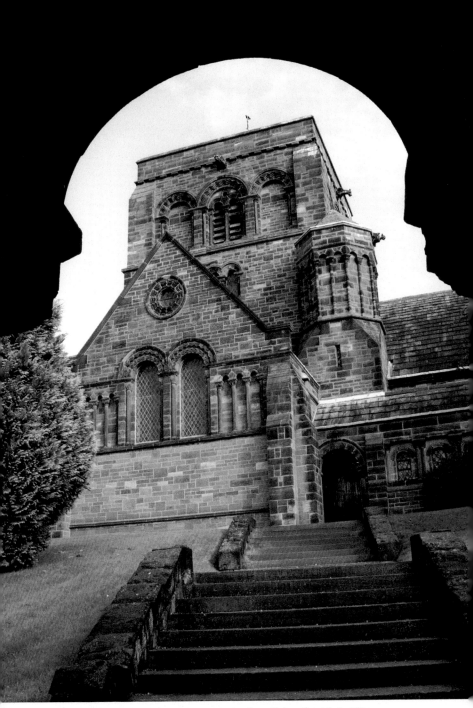

Thornton Hough's Norman-style church (walks 10 & 11)

A typical footpath in central Wirral

The old sea front in Parkgate (walk 12)

Heather flourishes in Wirral's pockets of lowland Heath

Autumn colours at Dibbinsdale (walk 17)

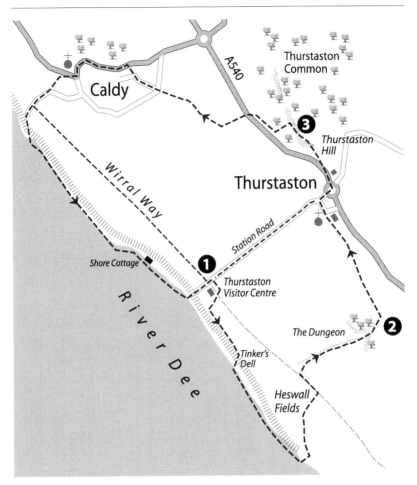

Turn right and continue to the Wirral Way. Turn left along the old track bed and after about 200m bear right (signed to the 'The Dungeon' FP 72) down the bank to follow a surfaced path ahead between fields. Follow the path beside a stream to a small wooded ravine, known locally as 'The Dungeon'. As you enter the woods bear left over a wooden footbridge and ascend wooden steps to the top of the wooded slope. Bear right now following waymarks to pass above a small waterfall and continue beside the stream to a T junction.

2. Turn left here (FP43) and follow the obvious path to Thurstaston church.

At the road continue straight ahead and take the first road on the right beyond the church. (To shorten the walk, don't turn right, continue along 'Station Road' back to point 1.)

At the busy A540 roundabout, cross over and turn left passing the 'Cottage Loaf'. Just after the pub bear right through a gate into Thurstaston Common (sign 'Public Footpath to Royden Park'). Follow the obvious path ahead passing a small school on the right. Shortly after this, and immediately before a tarmac road, turn sharp left onto a broad sandy path which rises to the top of Thurstaston Hill, highest point on the common.

At 255 feet, Thurstaston Hill is not the highest point in Wirral, but it undoubtedly has one of the finest panoramas. A view finder near the highest point identifies major landmarks and was erected in 1942 by Liverpool and District Federation of the Ramblers Association in honour of Andrew Blair, their founder member. An inscription reads: 'In honour of Andrew Blair F.R.G.S founder of the Federation in 1923 and to commemorate his work for those who walk in and enjoy the British countryside.' He also wrote several guide books for walkers.

The view on a clear day takes in much of Wirral and North Wales. Below to the west, green fields sweep down from Thurstaston to the marshes and shallow waters of the River Dee, while the dark silhouettes of the Clwydian Range stand proudly beyond. If you are lucky, the higher peaks of Snowdonia and the Great Orme will just be visible. Further north the wooded slopes of Caldy Hill act as a barrier to the urban sprawl of eastern Wirral where fields and woods give way to houses, factories, pylons and motorways. Beyond is the Lancashire coast and the Liverpool skyline dominated by its two cathedrals. Had it not been for the foresight of Birkenhead Town Council, who purchased Thurstaston Common as far back as 1879 for 'the benefit of the neighbourhood' and 'convenience of the inhabitants', this bit of greenery may well have disappeared beneath bricks and mortar decades ago.

3. From the triangulation pillar follow the well worn path northwest (in the direction of Caldy Hill and the mouth of the Dee estuary) soon passing a bench over to the left. About 50m further on there are two more benches. Turn left onto the visible path between the two benches. At a fork bear right down towards the road. At a path junction lower down turn left, soon walking parallel to the road below a stone wall. At the end of the wall go through a gap onto the road. (A540)

Cross the road and turn left. In about 50m turn right onto a signed footpath (FP 15). Walk ahead along the field edge and turn right through a small gate in the far corner. Follow the path between horse paddocks to cross a stile onto an access track and follow the track ahead.

At the road continue straight ahead ('Long Hey Road') and after 150m, where the road bears left (below a telegraph pole), take the enclosed footpath ahead. At the end of the path turn left along the road and continue to Caldy village.

Where the road bends to the right near a stone memorial in front of the church and about 30m after 'Croft Drive', bear left

The beach at Thurstaston

onto a signed bridleway. The bridleway follows a driveway at first ('The Croft'), then becomes a narrow sandy path between large wooded gardens. Follow the path to the road ('Croft Drive'), turn right and continue down to the sea front.

If the tide permits bear left and follow the sandy shore. In about a mile you will pass a cottage on the sand known as 'Shore Cottage'.

The origin of this cottage is unknown for sure but it is thought to have been built for the customs officers of the nearby port of Dawpool. The sandstone blocks scattered about the high tide mark are thought to be the remains of the quay, built in the eighteenth century to attract some of the sea trade which had abandoned Neston and Parkgate.

Today you would be lucky to float anything larger than a canoe in these shallow waters and in some ways this has been a blessing. We need only look to the nearby ports of Liverpool and Birkenhead, to see what might have been.

If the water is high, return by means of the Wirral Way to complete the walk.

Following the beach near 'Shore Cottage'

Thurstaston Hill & Irby

Distance: *4¼ miles/7km*

A walk through the woods and lowland heath of Thurstaston Common, with a return by green lanes and Irby village. Excellent, well-used footpaths throughout.

Start: There is a large public car park at Thurstaston Common Local Nature Reserve, just north of the 'Cottage Loaf' pub on the A540.
Grid ref: 246 846 (Landranger 108, Explorer 266).

The walk

1. Take one of the sandy paths which leave the back of the car park and rise through the heather and gorse to the triangulation pillar on Thurstaston Hill.

The hill is a popular spot and a fine day will find its network of sandy paths busy with visitors. It was secured as public open space by Birkenhead Town Council as far back as 1879 and has now been designated as both a Site of Special Scientific Interest and a Local Nature Reserve.

It is a fine example of a lowland heath and has a varying range of habitats for both animal and plant life. The drier ground has been colonised by heather and bilberry, while the damper hollows support cotton grass and mosses. A host of birds, including woodpecker, tawny owl, jay and nuthatches can also be found here.

The highest point, at 255 feet, is marked by the usual Ordnance Survey triangulation pillar and being largely clear of trees offers a fine panorama over much of northern Wirral and North Wales. A view finder erected in memory of Andrew Blair, founder of Liverpool and District Ramblers Association and author of several footpath guides, gives details of major landmarks and distances.

From the viewfinder take the broad sandy path to the north-west (in the direction of Caldy Hill and the mouth of the Dee estuary) which passes seats to run along the top of small crags and flat rocks overlooking sports fields away to the left. Futher on the woods become thicker but the path remains obvious—keep on the path straight ahead ignoring minor paths on either side.

Eventually you reach the corner of the common where an enclosed footpath bears to the left beside a sandstone wall. Go through a gap in the wall ahead and turn right. Stay beside the sandstone wall on one side or the other depending on which side has the best path. There are several breaks in the wall and large sections are missing altogether, but its line (directly ahead) can be followed quite easily. It separates the common from Royden Park and Hill Bark, the large rambling mansion of Sir Ernest Royden, hidden from view over on the left.

Thurstaston Hill

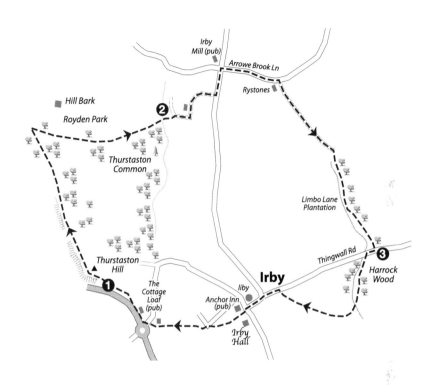

This *magnificent house sits comfortably in Royden Park, an area of wooded knolls and open grass adjoining the common and has been described as 'one of the most notable Victorian essays in half-timbered design anywhere in the country'. Parts of the building are modelled on Little Moreton Hall near Congleton, one of the best examples of an Elizabethan half-timbered hall in the country.*

Incredibly, the entire building was moved from its original location on Bidston Hill—where it was known as 'Bidston Court'—and re-erected here by Sir Ernest Royden in 1930. The reason for this drastic measure is plain enough if you compare the view from the present location with that from Bidston Hill. Even in the 1930s, the 40 years since its construction had seen the nearby suburbs of Birkenhead engulf much of the surrounding countryside.

When Sir Ernest died in 1960, Hill Bark was purchased by Hoylake Urban District Council who converted it into a home for the elderly. The grounds—Royden Park—are now open to the public.

Continue past a large wall-enclosed field on the left (part of Royden Park) and keep ahead again following the line of the missing wall. Soon it appears again with a field and large house on the left.

2. At the end of the wall you drop to a stream and footbridge. Climb the wooden steps beyond the bridge and follow the sandy path straight ahead (ignore the path to the left). At a T junction with a rough access road and a cottage to the right, turn right. Follow the access road, bearing left at a junction of paths/bridleways, and pass cottages and bungalows on the left. A little further on keep right at a fork and continue to the road.

Turn left at the road and at a small traffic island, beside 'Irby Mill' public house, turn right ('Arrowe Brook Lane'). Follow the road for about 400m before turning right into a signed bridleway just beyond a house ('Rystones'). Follow the bridleway (ignoring a permissive path on the left), which eventually runs into woods, for about ¾ mile to a road.

3. At the road cross over, turn right and after about 30m enter woods on the left. Follow the footpath through the trees and beside a small stream before leaving the woods by a small gate. Turn right here, cross the stream by stone steps and a kissing gate and walk ahead up the following field towards Irby. Keep to the right-hand side of the field and join an enclosed footpath on the right which leads to the road near the centre of Irby.

Turn left here and walk through Irby village to a T junction with the 'Anchor Inn' pub on the right and Irby Hall to the left.

The present hall dates from the seventeenth century and, until its reconstruction in 1888, was completely half-timbered. It stands on the site of the ancient manor house, given to the monks of St. Werburgh's in Chester in 1093, as a venue for their courts in Wirral. The earthworks,

Hill Bark

which are still clearly visible and must have originally surrounded the site, are probably the remains of a moat from the medieval period.

Throughout the Middle Ages, Wirral's close proximity to North Wales, along with the ease with which the shallow waters of the River Dee could be crossed, made it vulnerable to attacks by the Welsh.

Take the field path ahead and immediately opposite, signed to 'Thurstaston'. At the end of the first field bear right into 'Dawlish Road' and take the signed footpath between gardens on the left. Turn right behind the gardens and at the end of the path cross a stile. Walk through the centre of a small field to a large house. Bear left over a stile approximately 30m before buildings and pass between the house and outbuildings, and walk down the drive to the road. Turn left, then right at the A540 roundabout passing the 'Cottage Loaf' pub. Bear left into Thurstaston Common at a gate and at a fork bear left to return to the car park to complete the walk.

Arrowe Park
& Irby

Distance: *5½ miles/9km*

A walk through the woods of Arrowe Park and the lowland heath of Thurstaston Common. Excellent, well used footpaths throughout.

Start: There is ample parking in Arrowe Park, off Arrowe Brook Road, between Woodchurch and Greasby.
Grid ref. 265 868 (Ordnance Survey Explorer 265).

The Walk

1. Go through the large gate towards the back of the car park and follow the broad path into the woods. Bear left at a T junction in about 40m and follow the broad, straight tarmac path through the woods with the stream (Arrowe Brook) over to the right.

About 50m before the path leaves the woods to enter a large open playing field, bear right onto a narrow footpath. Follow this over a footbridge to a lake. Immediately before the lake there is a path junction. Turn right here through the trees and go through a kissing gate into fields. Turn right to the field corner, then go left up the field edge. Cross the stile in the corner and continue ahead to the road. Turn left along the road. Take care here, the road can be busy. After the bend the verge is wide enough to walk on. Continue to the small roundabout with the 'Irby Mill' pub on the right.

Go ahead along 'Hillbark Road'. Pass the houses ('The Farmhouse' and 'The Barn') on the right and take the signed footpath

The ornamental lake in Arrowe Park

on the left (about 50m past the houses). The right of way follows the access road to 'Quarry Cottage' at first. Immediately before the house and garden, bear left onto a narrow footpath. At a crossing path, turn right down hill and follow the path through two small fields to a path junction in the far corner. Turn right here down wooden steps to cross a footbridge over the stream. Follow the broad footpath ahead beside a stone wall on the right. At the end of the wall keep ahead in the same direction to a second wall with an open grass area beyond on the right. Continue with the wall on the right.

2. At the end of the wall (by the National Trust sign and information board) turn left onto a broad, obvious footpath. Follow the path through the common, a mix of heather and woods.

It is a fine example of a lowland heath and has a varying range of habitats for both animal and plant life. The drier ground has been colonised

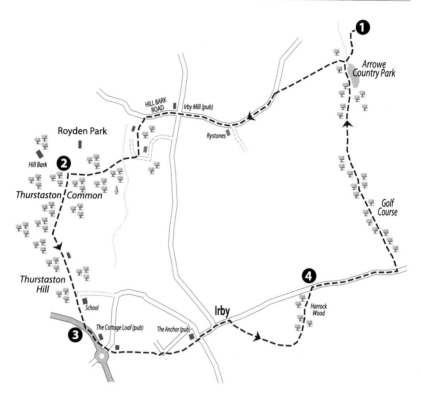

by heather and bilberry, while the damper hollows support cotton grass and mosses. A host of birds, including woodpecker, tawny owl, jay and nuthatches can also be found here. Go through a kissing gate beside a large gate and continue ahead on an improving track with fields on the left. Pass 'Benty Farm' and in about 100m or so, bear right onto a narrow woodland footpath (beneath overhead cables).

At the end of the path a kissing gate leads into a lane. Go ahead where lane becomes a sandy track passing a school on the left. Continue to the road. (Thurstaston Hill can be reached by footpaths on the right).

3. Turn left along the road and pass the 'Cottage Loaf' pub. At the roundabout just after the pub, turn left, cross the road and take the signed footpath on the right between stone houses. The right of way follows a driveway between cottages on the left and a barn on the right, then becomes fenced to reach a stile into a field. Bear right through the field passing a pond to cross a footbridge and stile. Follow an enclosed footpath which runs beside gardens turning left at the end to reach a housing estate ('Dawlish Road'). Turn right into a turning area to join a second footpath which again leads beside gardens and into a small field. Keep left along the field edge to the road near the centre of Irby with the 'Anchor Inn' pub to the left. Cross the road and walk ahead through the centre of Irby

Immediately after the shops take the signed footpath on the right. This follows an access road at first, then a short footpath ahead between hedges to enter fields again. Bear left along the field edge. At the bottom of the field go through a kissing gate and cross the stream. In 10m or so turn left into 'Harrock Wood', a narrow finger of National Trust woodland. A good path leads through the woods beside the stream.

4. At the road cross over and turn right along the wide grass verge. Ignore a permissive footpath between hedges on the left after the first field, continuing ahead past a cul-de-sac of houses on the left ('Parkway') and turn left into Arrowe Park (op posite 'Thingwall Drive') where there is a small parking area. Bear left at the back of the parking area through a kissing gate onto a good footpath. Follow this path along the left edge of the woods.

In a little under ½ mile the path turns right along a wooden walkway and over a footbridge to reach a path junction. Turn left here and follow the broad footpath through the woods. Pass the lake seen earlier continuing ahead crossing the footbridge over the stream to join a tarmac footpath. Turn left and follow this path back to the car park to complete the walk.

Heswall Dales & The Dungeon

Distance: *4½ miles/7km*

A walk that takes you from the marshy foreshore of the River Dee to the sandstone gorge of The Dungeon and through the tiny lowland heath of Heswall Dales, with a return along the marshes. Footpaths are good but the sections along the marshes are usually wet and muddy requiring suitable footwear.

Start: There is a sizable public car park situated at the end of 'Banks Road', Heswall.
Grid ref: 255 815 (Landranger 108, Explorer 266).

The walk

1. Turn left out of the car park and follow the lane down to the shore, now a mixture of sand, mud and salt marsh.

The fine sandy beach which graced the shore until about 30 years ago has all but disappeared, although small pockets of sand remain here and there and, unlike Parkgate, water still fills the little creek where boats await the incoming tide.

This change is part of a process which has transformed over half the estuary into dry land in less than three centuries. Man has helped nature here though with his canals, seawalls and reclamation schemes.

Two thousand years ago the River Dee provided Chester with a vital link to the sea. Roman and medieval troop ships came this way and when in later years the estuary began to silt up, threatening Chester's existence as a port, traders built a series of anchorages along Wirral's coast to continue their activities.

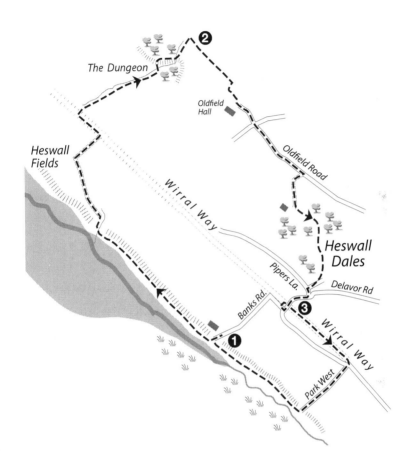

During the seventeenth and eighteenth centuries however, sea trade was finally strangled. Today the River Dee is of national importance to the many species of sea birds which winter here or rest in spring and autumn on their long migratory flights between the Arctic and Africa.

Turn right and make your way along the shore for just over ½ mile (this may not possible during very high tides).

Beyond a sea defence created from large white stones, and immediately after a stream which flows across the beach, turn right up a sandy path. Follow the main path ahead ignoring a left fork into 'Heswall Fields', a field of National Trust land to the left. Ignore a crossing path continuing ahead between fields to a eventually reach a T junction.

Turn right and continue to the Wirral Way. At the Wirral Way turn left and in about 200m bear right (signed to the 'The Dungeon' FP 72) down the bank to follow a surfaced path between fields. The path leads to a small wooded ravine, known locally as 'The Dungeon'. As you enter the woods bear left over a wooden footbridge and ascend wooden steps to the top of the slope. Bear right now following waymarks to pass above a small waterfall and continue beside the stream to a T junction with footpath 43.

2. Turn right here and follow the obvious path with fine views over the River Dee to the Welsh hills.

At the end of the path follow a farm track past Oldfield Hall on the right to reach 'Oldfield Road'.

It was at this old manor house that Sir Rowland Stanley, one of the most celebrated Cheshire knights of Queen Elizabeth's reign, spent his remaining years. An inscription above the door reads 'R 1604 S'

The shore at Heswall

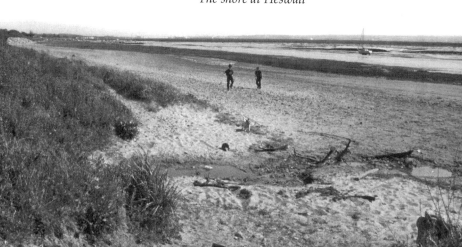

The shore at Heswall

*indicating a ten year stay. He died in 1614 at the ripe old age of 96;
quiet an achievement for the period in which he lived.*

Walk ahead along 'Oldfield Road'. In about 500m (after 'Oldfield Gardens'), turn right down a lane into 'Heswall Dales Local
Nature Reserve'. Lower down, bear left off the tarmac road immediately before a fruit growing field and follow a track beside
the field. Just before the track bears right to a farm, bear left onto
a bridleway which takes you through the reserve. Follow the
main path ahead enclosed by wooden fences and ignore minor
paths on either side.

*Like Thurstaston Common, this is a lowland heath and until about
40 years ago was almost treeless. Today however, the heather which
once covered the hillsides and valleys has almost disappeared. It has
been replaced by invasive birch and gorse which have colonised the area
as grazing has declined. As you walk through the reserve you will see
small pockets of heather which survive here and there.*

The path eventually leads into a cul-de-sac of bungalows. Turn right and at the end of the road ('Bushway') turn left ('Pipers Lane'). Almost immediately, turn right into 'Delavor Road'. Follow 'Delavor Road' over the Wirral Way, bearing right with the road.

3. To extend the walk taking in a section along the marshes, turn right through the large gate onto the Wirral Way before the road bends left (alternatively you can follow the road back to the car park for a shorter walk of 3½ miles). Turn right along the Wirral Way.

The Wirral Way was opened on 2nd October 1973 and follows the line of the old Hooton to West Kirby branch line. The last passenger train ran in 1956, although the line was not officially closed until 1962. The rails were removed in 1965.

Follow the Wirral Way under the 'Delavor Road' bridge and continue, passing under a second bridge in about 500m. Shortly, the path bends right to join a road as the next section of the old track bed has been built on. Cross over bearing right and walk down 'Park West' which leads down to the edge of the marshes ('Marine Drive'). Go down steps directly ahead onto the marshes and turn right on the footpath which leads back to 'Banks Road'. Turn right up the road and return to the car park to complete the walk.

(If the path along the marshes can not be walked for any reason return to the Wirral Way to reach Banks Road.)

Landican & Storeton

Distance: 4 miles/6.5km

An easy, almost level walk which explores the remaining greenery between Thingwall and the village of Storeton. Good footpaths throughout.

Start: Begin the walk in 'Landican Lane', Storeton. This links 'Little Storeton Lane' with 'Station Road' were there is a mini roundabout. Park in a small lay-by about half way along the lane. *Grid ref: 303 846 (Landranger 108, Explorer 266).*

The walk

1. A black and white fingerpost beside a stile indicates the start of the field path to 'Thingwall'. Cross the stile and follow the path through the centre of a large field and over the M53. Beyond the bridge the path continues ahead beside a fence. At the end of the fecne cross a farm track and take the path ahead crossing a brook by a small footbridge.

Continue straight ahead now through the centre of a second large field to a level crossing on the busy Birkenhead to Wrexham line (aim for the smaller of two pylons beside the track). Cross the track with caution (ignore paths on the left and right after the railway) continuing ahead along a footpath enclosed and overhung by hedges passing two sandstone gateposts. A little further on the path descends a wooded bank by steps to cross Prenton Brook by a footbridge. Beyond the brook bear half-right up a sloping field passing to the right a group of ponds to cross a stile by a gate into the next field. Go ahead up the following fields keeping to the right-hand field edges to enter an enclosed footpath by a stile. Follow this path until it eventually bends right to join a rough lane. Turn left and follow the lane to a T junction beside 'Woodfinlow Cottage'. Turn right along the lane.

You will find nothing at nearby Thingwall to suggest its past importance as the centre of Norse settlement in Wirral. From those early days only the name remains, but from this we know that it was used as the meeting place of the Norse 'thing' or parliament. This would probably have been on a nearby hilltop such as Cross Hill, although the exact location is unknown. Thingwall shares its name with Dingwall in Scotland and Tynwald in the Isle of Man.

2. At a sharp left-hand bend by a caravan storage area, take the signed ('Landican') footpath over the stile straight ahead. In about 30m turn right and walk through the caravans. After about 150m,

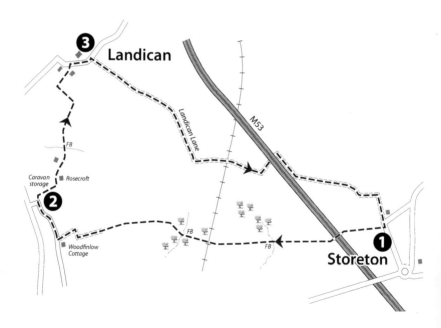

The quiet hamlet of Landican

immediately before a gate, turn left at a stile and walk along a short enclosed footpath. After two kissing gates either side of an access road (chalet on the right—'Rosecroft') , bear half-right and walk through a field beside the fence to a stile. Cross the stream and stile and continue along field edges with the familiar Liverpool/Birkenhead skyline ahead.

At the head of the field turn left through a gate and keep ahead to join a farm track which swings right past a farm and onto a quiet lane at Landican.

Landican is one of Wirral's forgotten corners. The tide of new housing which has engulfed so many of its pretty villages has not yet reached this quiet hamlet. As a result, the collection of ancient farms and cottages still sit comfortably amid green fields and quiet lanes—a reminder of what much of Wirral was like a century ago.

The name Landican is of British origin, from the Welsh 'llan' —a church foundation and common place name element throughout Wales, and 'Tegan'—*possibly an early Welsh saint. Other forms of the name exist in Llandegan and Capel Degan in Pembroke. Here in Wirral it is a remnant of the occupation of Wirral by British or Celtic tribes who were displaced by Saxons during the seventh century. The whole of Cheshire was occupied by the British until they came into contact with the expanding Saxon kingdom of Northumbria. An army under the command of the Northumbrian king defeated the Celts at the Battle of Chester in AD 616. Following this defeat, the Saxons were quick to colonise the area with the result that almost all settlement names in the county are now of Saxon origin. The survival of a few Welsh names in Wirral indicate that the Welsh remained here longer than the rest of Cheshire.*

3. Turn right and follow the lane for about 150m before turning into a green lane on the right, signed 'Public Bridleway to Storeton 1½ miles' (cycleway 56). Follow the lane for about ¾ mile, ignoring a path on the left, passing beneath both the railway and the M53. Follow the lane back to Storeton to complete the walk.

Storeton Hill

Distance: *6½ miles/10.5km*

A walk along quiet lanes and through the estate land around village of Brimstage, with a return through the woods of Storeton Hill.

Start: There is space for parking one or two cars just off the road in the centre of Storeton almost opposite 'Red Hill Road'. *Grid ref: 306 843 (Landranger 108, Explorer 266).*

The walk

1. From the parking area take the unsurfaced access road marked by a fingerpost ('Public footpath to Brimstage'). At the end of the road pass 'Lodge Farm' on the right and enter fields ahead by a kissing gate. Walk straight ahead through the centre of the field to a stile in the far corner by the motorway. In the next field walk parallel to the motorway to reach 'Brimstage Lane'.

Turn right under the motorway and follow the lane to the village of Brimstage (about ½ mile).

2. At 'Brimstage Road' cross over and turn left. In about 60m or so take the signed footpath into fields on the right. After the first field cross an access road by two stiles and continue ahead through the following fields on a good path. Cross a tree-lined driveway (one of the Leverhulme estate roads) taking the footpath opposite. The path cuts directly through the centre of the following field to enter a sunken footpath between hedges. Turn left along the path.

At the end of the path bear right to a junction of estate roads. Walk ahead over the first crossing road and in about 40m bear right with the track. Follow the track until you are within 100m of houses ahead. Take the signed footpath on the left (there is also a signed footpath a few yards ahead on the right at this point) and follow the path along the field edge. In the bottom corner of the field bear right onto an enclosed footpath beside Claire House hospice.

At the road (B5136) turn left over the bridge, cross over and continue passing the garage on the left. Immediately after the garage the road swings left towards the motorway. Take the lane

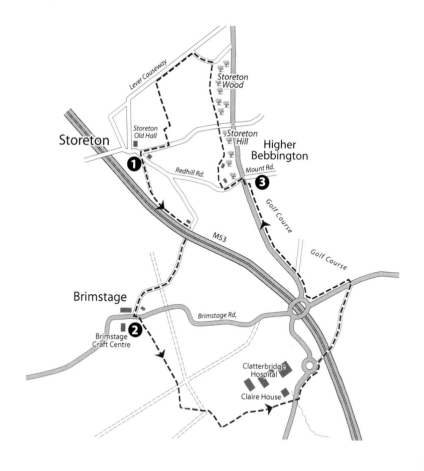

ahead which soon crosses over the motorway. At the T junction immediately after the bridge, turn left and follow the lane to its junction with the main road (B5137) on the outskirts of Bebbington.

Cross the main road by the crossing on the right and turn left along the paved path to the signed footpath on the right almost opposite the lane you have just walked down. Go through a gap in the hedge onto the golf course and turn left. The path passes through a small wood at first then continues parallel to the main road on the left around the edge of the golf course.

At a short crossing track, turn left passing a large gate to reach the road. Cross over and take the signed footpath opposite. Like the previous path, this follows the edge of the golf course passing through woods here and there for about ¾ mile.

At the end of the golf course there is a sandstone wall with a car park beyond and stone steps at its right and left end. Pass to the left of this through the trees to reach the corner of the wall separating the woods from the main road and cross the steps to reach the road.

Storeton village

3. This is 'Mount Road' and 'Redhill Road' should be directly opposite. Cross over and walk down 'Redhill Road'. Pass 'Rake Hey' on the right and just before the lane bends right, turn right onto the signed 'Public Footpath to Rest Hill Road' (FP 59), immediately to the left of a driveway. Follow the enclosed footpath beside two houses and gardens to join a track below the woods of Storeton Hill. Turn left along the track and continue to the road ('Rest Hill Road').

Cross the road and go through the gate directly opposite into Storeton Wood. Follow the obvious broad raised footpath which runs straight ahead.

This path follows the line of the 'Storeton Tramway' used between 1838 and 1905 to transport stone to a jetty on Bromborough Pool, when the nearby quarries were worked for their excellent building stone. Many local buildings were built with stone from here including Birkenhead Town Hall and Birkenhead Priory.

There is evidence to suggest that stone has been taken from this hillside since Roman times. Several inscribed and sculptured stones held by the Grosvenor Museum in Chester are believed to have come from Storeton. One of the finest examples is the tomb of a Roman centurion of the Fifth Legion, which can be dated to AD 44.

Where the line of the tramway curves right towards the quarries, keep straight ahead on the path marked by red horseshoes. This eventually leads to a gate out of the woods and into a lane. Turn left along the lane and at the T junction ('Lever Causeway'), turn left again.

Walk along the wide grass verge for about 500m to a stile and fingerpost (just before the 30 mph limit sign) leading into fields on the left. This section of the walk passes through horse paddocks where there are nearly always horses. (If you are nervous around horses this section can be missed out by continuing along the road back to Storeton.) Turn left over the stile and walk ahead to a stile by a gate. Go over the stile and keep ahead beside the hedge on the right. At the far end of the field two stiles take you

over a broad farm track and into a large field again. Keep beside
the right-hand hedge until a stile takes you into 'Rest Hill Road'.

Turn right along the road to return to Storeton village.

Storeton today has little more than a handful of cottages and farms
and has neither church nor public house. In the past however, it was a
centre of some importance. Storeton Hall was the residence of Wirral's
Master Foresters when it became a royal hunting forest in the twelfth
century. Alan Sylvester, the first Master Forester, was granted land
at Storeton, Hooton and Puddington by Ranulf II, the fourth Norman
Earl of Chester, about 1130, along with the Wirral Horn as a symbol
of his office.

He was expected to enforce the strict Forest Laws which protected
local game animals and the vegetation which gave them cover for the
king's hunt. The agricultural needs of the local population were placed in
low priority, with the result that the Forest Laws were very unpopular,
even with the local gentry. The job of the Master Forester must always
have been a difficult and dangerous one, although Wirral's forest did not
last long—it was the first of Cheshire's royal hunting forests to be 'dis-
saforested' (i.e. the Forest Laws were removed) in 1376 by Edward III.

The ancient gable and high pointed window which can be seen form-
ing part of the farm buildings at Storeton Hall Farm, is the remains of
the fourteenth century hall of William Stanley, one of the later Master
Foresters. The old horse tracks which the foresters used to reach distant
parts of Wirral have formed the basis of the local road and footpath
network although one of these ancient routes has survived almost in
its original form and is known locally as the 'Roman Road'. The path
leads north towards Prenton and is paved with heavy sandstone slabs.
Its age is unknown for sure but it is almost certain to have been laid
during the Middle Ages to aid the crossing of one of the marshy hollows
which surround Storeton.

Brimstage & Thornton Hough

Distance: *3 miles/4.75km*

A short, easy and completely level walk through the estate land of the Lever family. Brimstage Hall and Craft Centre and café is visited at the mid point of the walk making it suitable for the very young or elderly.

Start: Cars can be parked at a number of locations around Thornton Hough. Begin the walk beside 'The Seven Stars' public house in the centre of the village.
Grid ref: 305 810 (Landranger 108, Explorer 266).

The walk

1. Cross the road and take the signed footpath ('Public Footpath to Brimstage') to the right of Thornton Hough Primary School (just after the phone box). Follow the right of way along an access road to a T junction. Turn right here and in about 60m, turn left onto an enclosed footpath which shortly runs into fields. The path is easily followed now through the fields ahead crossing one of the tree-lined driveways to Thornton Manor, home of Lord Leverhulme (over to the left).

Thornton Manor was the home of William Hesketh Lever, the first Viscount Leverhulme, who came to Wirral in 1887 to begin soap manufacture at Port Sunlight. The large Victorian mansion set in beautiful countryside away from the sights and smells of the soap industry obviously appealed to him and after an initial period of renting, he bought the manor outright in 1891. He was a lover of building and in the following years transformed it into the grand Elizabethan-style residence that we see today.

Cross the driveway and go through the kissing gate opposite. Walk ahead through two more fields to cross a stile into an enclosed footpath. Ignoring the path to the right, follow the path straight ahead to the road.

2. Turn right at the road and right again in a few yards along the main road (A5137 'Brimstage Road'). Where the road turns sharp left take the path (FP 25) on the right (straight ahead as you approach) which cuts through fields to Brimstage Hall and Craft Centre.

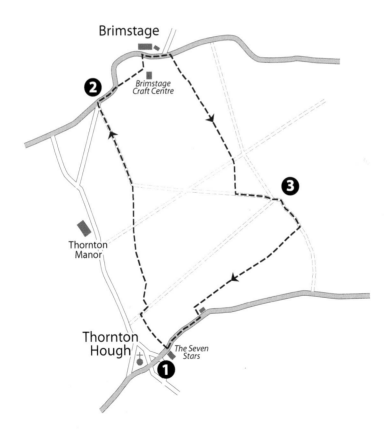

Brimstage Hall in 1903, from the book, 'Picturesque Cheshire'

The hall's most interesting and unique feature is the ancient stone tower which adjoins the main building. Although the date of its construction is unknown for sure, it is considerably older than the hall itself and was known to have been in existence in 1398. In that year Sir Hugh de Hulse and his wife Margery obtained a licence to build an oratory in the base of the tower which still exists. The tower obviously predates this, making it one of the oldest buildings in Wirral.

Some have suggested that the tower is a remnant of a much larger stronghold, but the evidence seems to indicate that it was never more than a tower house or pele tower. Its use as a stronghold is clear both from its siting—on a slight rise with evidence of a moat—and in the construction of slit windows for archers and provision for pouring molten lead onto attackers.

The Domvilles originally held Brimstage but it passed to the de Hulse family with the marriage of Margery Domville and Sir Hugh de Hulse mentioned previously. In 1440 Sir John Troutbeck, later killed at the battle of Blore Heath in 1459, married the heiress and the lands passed to the Troutbecks. Remnants of the coat-of-arms of both these ancient families are carved into parts of the tower.

Walk straight ahead through the car park and bear left down the short drive to the road. Turn right along the road and after 200m turn right again into fields, signposted 'Public Footpath Thornton Hough'. After the first field cross an access road by two stiles and continue ahead through the following fields on a good path. Cross a tree-lined driveway (one of the Leverhulme estate roads) taking the footpath opposite. The path cuts directly through the centre of the following field to enter sunken footpath between hedges. Turn left along the path

3. At the end of the path bear right to a junction of estate roads. Walk ahead over the first crossing road and in about 40m bear right with the track. Follow the track until you are within 100m or so of houses ahead. Take the signed field path on the right here. Follow the path ahead through three large fields to enter a short driveway behind houses on the left. Turn left down the driveway to the road. At the road turn right and walk back to Thornton Hough to complete the walk.

Thornton Hough & Raby

Distance: *5¼ miles/8.5km*

Easy, straightforward walking along lanes and field paths through the estate land of the Lever family. There is a section along a main road which can not be avoided although there is a good pavement. Don't miss a visit to the Wheatsheaf Inn at Raby towards the end of the walk.

Start: Cars can be parked at a number of locations around Thornton Hough. There is a small car park beside toilets by the sports fields. Begin the walk beside 'The Seven Stars' public house in the centre of the village.
Grid ref: 305 810 (Landranger 108, Explorer 266).

The walk

1. Cross the road and take the signed footpath ('Public Footpath to Brimstage') to the right of Thornton Hough Primary School (just after the phone box). Follow the right of way along an access road to a T junction. Turn right here and in about 60m, turn left onto an enclosed footpath which shortly runs into fields. The path is easily followed through the fields ahead crossing one of the tree-lined driveways to Thornton Manor, home of Lord Leverhulme (over to the left).

Thornton Manor was the home of William Hesketh Lever, the first Viscount Leverhulme, who came to Wirral in 1887 to begin soap manufacture at Port Sunlight. The large Victorian mansion set in beautiful countryside away from the sights and smells of the soap in-

dustry obviously appealed to him and after an initial period of renting, he bought the manor outright in 1891. He was a lover of building and in the following years transformed it into the grand Elizabethan-style residence that we see today.

Cross the drive and go through the kissing gate opposite. Walk ahead through two more fields to cross a stile into an enclosed footpath. Ignoring the path to the right, follow the path straight ahead to the road.

2. Turn left at the lane and follow it to a T junction. Go ahead here on the signed path with Thornton Manor on the left. Soon

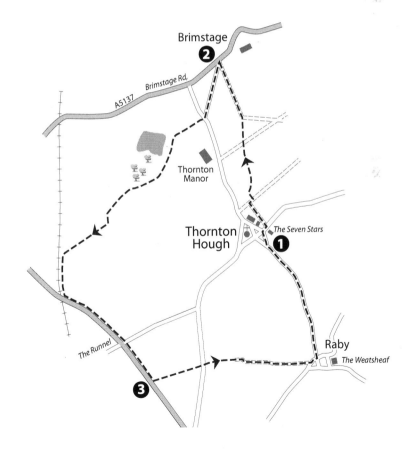

Thornton Hough

the path enters woods and you will get glimpses of a large lake through the trees on your right, part of Thornton Manor estate. After the woods follow a fenced footpath ahead with a field on the left, before entering woods again. Pass beneath a large pylon and continue ahead through a strip of woodland for about ½ mile.

At the end of the wood by the railway, turn left over a stile into a field and walk ahead along the field edge (railway to the right). In the bottom corner of the field bear left again to exit the field in the far corner to reach the main road.

This is the A540 and a short section along this busy highway can not be avoided. It is best to cross over and use the path on the far side. Turn left along the footpath passing houses on the right, then a lane ('The Runnell') also on the right. Continue ahead on the footpath separated from the road by a wide verge and trees.

3. In about 500m look for a signed footpath on the opposite side of the road. Cross the road and follow the path ahead through a strip of woodland to a road (B5136). Cross the road and take the signed footpath opposite beside 'Yew Tree Farm' on the right. Follow the enclosed footpath ahead to the road on the edge of Raby village (about ½ mile).

(If you enjoy a good country pub, Wheatsheaf Inn, just along the lane in Raby, makes a welcome diversion here.)

At the road turn left then left again along 'Raby Road' to return to Thornton Hough. As you enter the village bear right by the church along 'Church Road' to return to 'The Seven Stars' to complete the walk.

Thornton Hough owes much of its present appearance to Lord Leverhulme who practically rebuilt it when he bought nearby Thornton Manor in the 1890s. The neo-Elizabethan style which he chose for Thornton Manor can also be seen in the attractive half-timbered cottages which surround the green. The parish church has the curious distinction of having a five-faced clock and the second church was built by Leverhulme in the Norman style.

The Wheatsheaf, Raby

Parkgate

Distance: *4 miles/6km or 5½miles/9km*

Easy, level walking along the old sea front of this one-time sea bathing resort and seaport. Return is made by a section of the Wirral Way. Footpaths are generally good, although a short section of path along the marshes may be muddy at times.

Start: Ample free parking is available at the Old Baths car park at the northern end of the old sea front ('The Parade'). The car park is approached by a short road adjacent to 'The Boat House' pub. *Grid ref: 274 790 (Landranger 117, Explorer 266).*

The walk

1. Walk back along the access road to pass 'The Boat House' and walk ahead along Parkgate's old water front ('The Parade').

It is over half a century since the sea finally abandoned Parkgate, leaving the old cottages to look out onto acres of marsh grass where there had previously been bright yellow sand. It is hard to imagine just how much this landscape has changed in the last three centuries.

In its heyday Parkgate was a bustling seaport of national importance. This was partly due to the Dublin Packet Service which ran on a demand basis for over 70 years with many famous passengers, among them Handel and John Wesley, making the sometimes hazardous crossing.

Parkgate eventually lost the Packet Service to Holyhead where a shorter and more reliable crossing could be obtained. This was partly due to the improved road travel through North Wales, along with the rapid silting of the River Dee which robbed the port of its navigable water. The last boat to land passengers here was in 1811.

This was not the end of Parkgate's prosperity however. The sands which had clogged the deep channel now attracted a new kind of visitor — the sea bather. Throughout the early decades of the nineteenth century, Parkgate was 'much resorted to by the gay and fashionable world'. The coming of the railways in later years took many of these visitors to other resorts, although locals continued to use the beach here until the 1940s when the marsh finally reached the sea wall.

Today you can barely see the sea from here, except on very rare occasions, however, we need only reflect on the fate of more prosperous ports — such as Holyhead, Liverpool and Birkenhead — who inherited much of Parkgate's trade to, see what Parkgate might have become.

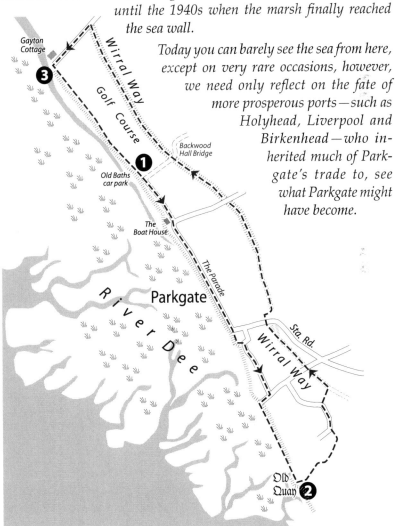

At the far end of 'The Parade' where the road turns left away from the marshes, continue straight ahead past the 'Old Quay' pub to join a narrow footpath that runs along the sandstone wall on the left, then passes between gardens. At the end of the path turn right and walk along a road with large houses on either side. At the end of the road follow the path ahead between driveways to a second road ('Manorial Road South'). Walk ahead to the end of the road where it turns sharp left, with 'Old Quay Close' ahead. Turn right here onto a footpath which leads down to the marsh edge. A good path goes left along the edge of the marshes now. Follow this path until it eventually bears left into a field.

The ruined sandstone walls which separate this field from the marshes are the remains of the Old Quay, a sixteenth century seaport. Today they are completely landlocked and look out onto acres of marsh grass where previously there had been enough water to take large sea-going ships.

The strange story of how the Old Quay lost both its water and its trade began in the mid-thirteenth century with the decline of the port of Chester due to 'the abundance of sands which had choked the creek'. As a result, anchorages were established downstream at Shotwick and Burton, but within a century these too had become choked. The 'New Key', as it was then called, was built here beside what was then a deep channel about 1550. After a number of problems associated with its building and funding it was replaced by a new port established at Parkgate. From then on it became known as the 'Old Quay' and gradually fell into ruins. The siltation of the river continued with the deep channel moving over to the Welsh side of the estuary. By the early 1920s, the sandy beach turned to mud and then disappeared beneath the spreading marsh grass.

Cross a stream and continue to a stile in the sandstone wall at the southern end of the Old Quay.

2. Don't cross the stile, instead turn left and follow a gravel footpath across fields to enter a narrow tarmac lane by a kissing gate. Go ahead along the lane for about 250m before taking an enclosed footpath on the right which shortly joins the Wirral Way. Turn left along the Wirral Way.

Eventually you reach a car park where a bridge once carried the railway over Station Road. Walk ahead down to the road, turn right for a few metres, then cross over and turn left into 'The Ropewalk'. Immediately before the first house on the right, take the footpath on the right which takes you back onto the Wirral Way. Follow the Wirral Way along the edge of Parkgate, crossing a bridge over the road, then passing under two bridges.

To shorten the walk leave the Wirral Way at the second bridge over the old track-bed (Backwood Hall Bridge). Go left up to a farm road, turn left and follow the track back to the car park. Alternatively, continue for a further ¾ mile to the third bridge at the end of the golf course. Go right up to the lane (Cottage Lane), turn left and walk down to the marsh edge at Gayton.

3. Turn left onto the shoreline footpath and follow this back to the car park to complete the walk.

Parkgate in the early 1900s

Neston

Distance: *4½ miles/7.25km*

An easy, level walk along a section of the Wirral Way and the old sea shore to the site of an Elizabethan seaport and the more recent quays associated with local coal mining. Excellent paths throughout although the section along the marsh can be muddy at times.

Start: There is a sizable car park provided for the Wirral Country Park in 'Lees Lane', Neston, just off the A540.
Grid ref: 306 775 (Landranger 117, Explorer 266).

The walk

1. Walk through the picnic area which adjoins the car park and turn left along the Wirral Way. Just before the first bridge, bear right down steps onto a farm track and turn right. Follow the track ('Cuckoo Lane'), which rises gently between fields, before turning right. In about 175m, at a junction of paths, turn left onto a narrower footpath and follow this to a T junction with a bridleway. Turn right and walk along the bridleway to a school on the left with a housing estate opposite.

2. Bear left through a playing field adjacent to the school and cut through the centre of the following field. Turn right and join a short access road (Cumbers Lane) beside houses ('Cumbers Cottages'). At the road turn left and after a few metres bear right immediately after 'The Wheatsheaf' pub into 'Well Lane'.

This is the village of Ness, once described as 'one of the most miserable in the hundred, consisting of a mere mass of hovels inhabited

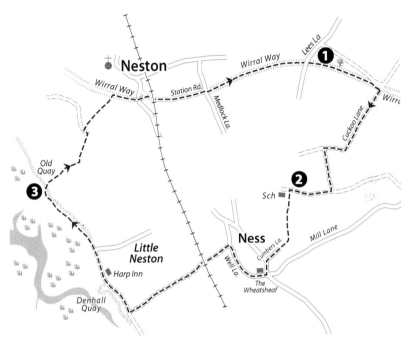

by colliers'. Today the scene is somewhat different although it is less recognisable as a separate village having been absorbed into the suburbs of nearby Neston.

Ness is perhaps best known for its botanic gardens originally laid out by Arthur Bulley, a Liverpool cotton merchant. Bulley delighted in the rare and unusual and financed several expeditions to China and the Himalayas which provided him with regular samples from these distant lands. When he died in 1942 his daughter gave the gardens to the University of Liverpool on condition that they remain open to the public.

Perhaps less well known is that Ness is the birth place of Lady Hamilton, the most famous beauty of her time and mistress of Lord Nelson. She was born Emma Lyon on the 26th April 1765 in a house which still stands and is now known as 'Swan Cottage'. After her father's death while still a baby, her mother moved to Harwarden where Emma grew up.

By the age of 17 she was working as a nursemaid in London where her striking beauty soon brought her to the notice of the rich and famous. Among these where several eminent portrait painters such as Gainsborough, Reynolds, Lawrence and Romney. Romney is said to have completed no fewer than twenty five portraits of her and regarded her as the 'perfection of feminine beauty'.

She gained her greatest fame however by becoming the mistress of Lord Nelson and even appeared with him in public. After his death at Trafalgar she was forced to flea to Calais to escape debtor's prison where she died in poverty on 15th January 1815.

Follow the lane with houses and cottages on either side at first, before fields on the left allow a wide view over the River Dee towards North Wales. A little further on, turn left at a track (just before new bungalows and opposite 'Willow Croft') and follow this to eventually pass beneath the railway. Continue ahead for almost ½ mile until your each a T junction with a gravel access road near the edge of the marshes. Turn right and follow the road along the marsh edge to the 'Harp Inn'.

The remains of Denhall Quay are separated from the sea by over two miles of salt marsh

Miners at the Wirral Colliery in the 1920s

Just before the Harp Inn you will see the remains of Denhall Quay, built in the days when the water just a stone's throw from here was deep enough to accommodate large sea-going vessels. Today, these sandstone blocks are separated from the sea by almost two miles of marsh grass.

The quay was used primarily to ship coal from the nearby Wirral Colliery to Ireland, until the channel became too shallow for boats to dock here. It is quite well preserved and the majority of the sandstone blocks are still in place.

Further along the coast lie the spoil heaps of the Wirral Colliery which closed in 1928 after operating for 175 years. Here men and boys toiled in wet and dirty conditions to bring poor quality coal to the surface from nearly two miles beneath the estuary. The mines were so plagued by water, which seeped through the porous sandstone, that coal had to be transported along 'canals' or partly flooded shafts in small boats, before being hauled to the surface by hand.

Continue along the access road beyond the 'Harp Inn' and where this turns right into 'Marshlands Road', continue ahead on a farm track. Where the track ends, a path continues along the marsh edge to the remains of the Old Quay, once an important seaport.

The story of the Old Quay began in the thirteenth century when Chester began to lose its sea trade due to the silting up of the River Dee. As a result, anchorages were established down stream at Shotwick and Burton, but by the sixteenth century the water had become too shallow for ships of a reasonable size to dock there. The 'New Key', as it was then called, was built beside the deep channel at Neston around 1550, but problems with its funding and building meant that it was never a success and within a century it was replaced by a new port at Parkgate. From then on it became known as the 'Old Quay' and gradually fell into ruins. Today it is well and truely land locked, the ruined stone walls of the quay look out over almost two miles of salt marsh and grass.

3. Cross the stile in the sandstone wall and turn right onto a gravel footpath. Follow the path ahead through fields and over a wooden footbridge. The path eventually becomes enclosed by hedges. In a few metres and before you reach a kissing gate into a tarmac lane, turn right through a kissing gate and follow a path through two fields to the Wirral Way. Turn right here and follow the Wirral Way.

After a bridge over the road near the centre of Neston, the old track bed ends. Bear right here passing under a railway bridge and continue along the road ahead. At the end of the road at a T junction with 'Mellock Lane', cross over and join the old track bed again (opposite).

Follow the Wirral Way for about ¾ mile passing through a deep rock cutting. Beyond the cutting, pass beneath a road bridge ('Lees Lane') before bearing left into the picnic area to complete the walk.

Willaston

Distance: *5 miles/8km*

A level walk along green lanes, quiet roads and a section of the Wirral Way centred on the village of Willaston.

Start: Car parking is available for the Wirral Way on the outskirts of the village at Hadlow Station in 'Hadlow Road'. *Grid ref: 332 773 (Landranger 117, Explorer 266).*

The walk

1. Turn right out of the car park and walk along the road ('Hadlow Road') into the centre of Willaston. Turn left at the T junction ('Neston Road') and after about 100m, and immediately before the church, cross over and take the enclosed footpath beside the cemetery ('Village Walk'). At the corner of the cemetery turn left, then immediately right into 'Mill Green'. Immediately before the first house on the left, turn left onto a signed path between gardens which leads past 'Jacksons Pond' into playing fields. Keep along the right-hand field edges ahead to reach a quiet lane. Turn right and walk along the lane towards Willaston Mill.

The mill was built around 1800 by William Lightbound and replaced an earlier mill on the same site. It has the tallest tower in Wirral and was in regular use until 1930 when a violent storm destroyed the sails.

Just beyond the mill, look for a well used bridleway on the left adjacent to terraced houses, signed for 'Raby'. Follow this for almost 1 mile keeping left and ignoring other footpaths on the right.

2. At 'Willaston Road', turn left and follow the verge until the road bears to the left. Turn right here and in about 40m bear left onto a bridleway. Follow the bridleway to the road, turn right and after about 600m look for a signed field path on the left (about 25m after a signed footpath on the right). Keep to the field edge and at the busy A540 turn left. After about 80m turn right into 'Lees Lane' and continue to the Wirral Country Park car park.

3. Just before the car park turn left onto a bridleway which runs parallel to the Wirral Way for about 550m. Bear right up the bank to join the Wirral Way just before a stone bridge. Turn left over the bridge and follow the Wirral Way back to the car park at Hadlow Station to complete the walk.

Until the thirteenth century Willaston was known as 'Wilavestun' and was a settlement of some importance giving its name to the local hundred. This, along with its central location and large village green,

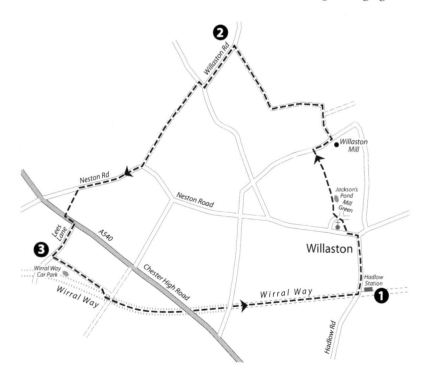

Willaston Mill

seem to indicate that it was used as a meeting place for the hundred and possibly the even older Anglo-Saxon communities prior to the Norman conquest.

Today there are many links with the past and a number of older buildings remain. Of particular note is the sixteenth century 'Ash Tree Farm' in 'Hadlow Road'. During renovation work, one of the massive oak timbers was found to contain a canon ball, indicating that it may have originally been taken from a ship wrecked on the nearby coast.

The half-timbered building now known as the 'Old Red Lion' (adjacent to the Memorial Hall) was formerly the 'Red Lion Inn', built in 1631 and mentioned in numerous nineteenth century guide books.

Also of note is the 'Old Hall' in 'Hadlow Road'. This late sixteenth or early seventeenth century brick and stone building has projecting gables in the form of a letter 'E' — possibly a tribute to Queen Elizabeth.

Shotwick & Puddington

Distance: 6½ miles/10.5km

Easy walking through farmland and quite lanes with occasional woodland centred on the hamlet of Shotwick — once a busy seaport, but now isolated by the modern road system and left high and dry by the receding river. There are some busy roads to cross on this walk requiring care.

Start: Begin the walk in Shotwick, situated in a cul-de-sac at the end of 'Shotwick Lane'. Park in a small lay-by in the lane just before the village.
Grid ref: 339 719 (Landranger 117, Explorer 266).

The walk

1. Walk back out of the village and turn left along 'Hall Lane' . Ignore a left turn almost immediately continuing ahead to pass Shotwick Hall.

The Hall was built in 1662 for Joseph Hockenhull and replaced an earlier fortified manor house which no longer stands. The moated site of this building is surrounded by trees in the fields opposite the Hall.

Immediately after the Hall, the lane becomes a farm track and after a couple of bends runs into fields. Follow the footpath directly ahead here between hedges. Go through a gate at the end of the path and walk along the left edge of two small fields. Two small gates lead into the third field and the path turns right up the field edge. When you are almost level with the first large pylon on the left, turn left through the centre of the field. Pass a pond (on the right) and bear half-right to the field corner (aim between a farm on the left and house on the right). In the next field keep ahead beside the left-hand hedge towards farm buildings. Immediately before the farm buildings turn right up a concrete farm road to the lane. Turn left along the lane.

Follow the lane to a T junction ('Puddington Lane').

To include a loop which takes in the village of Puddington turn left (alternatively, turn right here and walk along the lane for about ¾ mile and continue from point 2).

For the Puddington loop, look for a signed footpath on the left as you reach the first cottages. The right of way follows an access drive to its end, then bears right between fences and beside gardens.

Puddington Old Hall can be seen over to the left. The Hall, built in 1490, has been greatly altered over the centuries and as a result little of

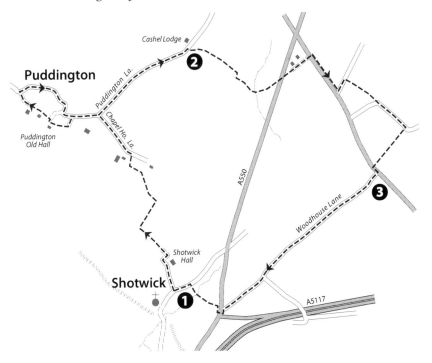

the original building remains, although traces of the moat remain. Of particular note are the remains of a dovecote built at a time when fresh winter meat was hard to come by. The keeping of pigeons in this way was a guarded privilege among the gentry and this dovecote is one of only two in Wirral, the other being at Gayton.

For over 500 years the manor was held by the Massey family, famed for their love of battle. Various members of this ancient family distinguished themselves fighting on both foreign and English soil. A tale of particular note concerns William Massey, who, in 1715 at the age of 60 joined the Pretender's forces at Preston. When they were overwhelmed by Royalists and surrendered, William fled to Puddington. He rode nonstop to Speke where he forced his exhausted steed across the Mersey almost at its widest point, gaining the far bank near Hooton. On reaching Puddington the beast collapsed and died and was buried where it fell.

William knew that home was not a safe haven however, and that he would soon be arrested and face execution. In a bid to create an alibi he had thrashed a local farmer on his return to the Hall and, knowing that he would be summoned to court, used this, along with his speedy return to prove that he could not have been in Preston on the day of the battle. This, it seems, did not help him, he was arrested shortly after and died in prison at Chester Castle in February 1716.

At the end of the fenced path turn right along the road, then left almost immediately along the drive to 'Old Hall Farm'. Immediately before you reach 'The Hayloft', a house on the left, take the enclosed footpath ahead. Go through a metal kissing gate at the end of the path and keep ahead through a farmyard to a second kissing gate which leads onto a farm access road. Walk ahead down the access road to the lane.

Turn right along the lane and soon you are back in the centre of Puddington beside the village green.

Walk back along the lane passing 'Chapel House Lane' used earlier on the right. Continue along Puddington Lane for about ¾ mile.

2. A few yards beyond the driveway to 'Cashel Lodge', a large, grand looking house on the left, look for a stile and footpath sign on the right leading into fields. Cross the stile and bear left around the edge of the field to a stile in the far corner. Go over the stile and keep ahead along the left-hand field edge turning right, then left with the fence/hedge. In the bottom corner of the field cross a grassy, overgrown bridge over Shotwick Brook and walk ahead beside the hedge to a kissing gate which leads abruptly onto the busy A550. **Take care** here, there is little or no verge, the road is very busy and traffic passes at high speed.

Bear left across the road to the stile and fingerpost marking the right of way, and walk through a small car park by workshops to a stile to the right of the buildings. Cross the stile and follow an enclosed footpath to a driveway by houses on the left. Walk ahead down the driveway to the A540.

Cross the road (another busy one with traffic moving at high speed!) and turn right along the footway. At 'Chapel Lane', immediately before the chapel, turn left and in about 150m take the signed footpath on the right. Walk ahead through a small field to a stile and footbridge, then ahead again along an enclosed path to the road. Go ahead along the road and at a sharp left-hand bend turn right over a stile onto a signed field path. Follow the footpath ahead through the fields to the A540 again. Turn left and in a few yards cross over and turn right along Woodbank Lane.

3. The noise of the main road soon fades as you head down this quiet lane, once a road of far greater importance leading to ancient fording points and the tidal roads across the Dee estuary into Wales.

Follow the lane to the road junction with the A550 where there is a crossing by traffic lights. It is best to use the crossing here as this is a fast road. Cross the road with care and turn right. In about 100m or so, take the signed footpath to 'Shotwick' on the left.

Go through the kissing gate and bear half-right through a field to a small gate in the corner. Go through the gate and a kissing

Shotwick Church

gate in a few metres leads into a sloping field on the left. Descend this field to a footbridge over the stream in the bottom right corner. Cross the footbridge and rise up the field to 'Shotwick Lane' to complete the walk.

Shotwick is quiet hamlet, hardly noticed by traffic on the busy Welsh road and lies almost forgotten, yet for centuries it stood on the main route from Wirral into North Wales. Before the River Dee around Sealand was reclaimed, a tidal road ran from the lane beside the church across the sands to Flint.

Earlier still, an anchorage was built here as a replacement for Chester, then suffering the effects of siltation. During the Middle Ages several armies sailed from Shotwick to battles in Ireland and North Wales, among them the famous Cheshire archers who are said to have practised their skills in the fields below the church. In later years anchorages were established at Burton, Neston and Parkgate as siltation of the river continued.

Today the swirling waters of the River Dee have become dry land, even the wild marshes have disappeared. In their place lie fields, hedges, cattle and sheep, and in more recent years, the monstrous buildings of the steel industry at Shotton. The only clue to earlier events is the almost artificially flat land between here and Flint and the nearby coastal step below the church (the old coastline).

With the tidal road across the marshes no longer in use, Shotwick lies frozen in time. Most of the old buildings date from the seventeenth century although one of the oldest is probably 'Greyhound Farm', previously the 'Greyhound Inn'. It was here in 1750 that three Irish labourers were arrested for beating and killing a fellow traveller on the nearby Chester Road. They were detained over night at Shotwick before being sent to jail at Chester Castle the following day. Two were found guilty, hanged at Broughton and their bodies 'hung up in irons near Two Mills on the heath, in the road to Parkgate'. Today, 'Gibbet Mill', which was built shortly afterwards, stands near the spot where they hung.

Shotwick & Shotwick Castle

Distance: *5 miles/8km*

Easy walking through farmland and quite lanes between the hamlet of Shotwick and the site of Shotwick Castle. Good footpaths throughout. Some unavoidable road sections.

Start: Begin the walk in Shotwick, situated in a cul-de-sac at the end of 'Shotwick Lane'. Park in a small lay-by in the lane just before the village.
Grid ref: 339 719 (Landranger 117, Explorer 266).

The walk

1. Walk down towards the church and go through the small gate immediately adjacent to the cemetery. Follow the old lane, cobbled here and there, past the church and out towards the old marshlands.

This old lane originally led down to the marshes and an ancient ford which led across the River Dee to Wales.

Continue along the lane crossing an old sandstone bridge over a stream (Shotwick Bridge) after which the lane bears right and heads out over what, 150 years ago, would have been tidal marshes similar to those at Parkgate today.

Continue to join a tarmac lane by houses on the right. Follow this lane as it bends right and passes under the expressway to reach a T junction ('Green Lane West'). Cross over here and turn left to the roundabout. Walk anti-clockwise (right) around the roundabout crossing over the dual carriageway and slip road and turn right into 'Green Lane East'. Follow the road as it curves right and take the first road on the left ('Green Lane East' again). In about 75m turn left into a tarmac cycle lane which runs tight below the expressway embankment.

In about 400-500m look for a metal kissing gate on the right immediately before a stream (the stream marks the border of England and Wales). Go through the kissing gate and follow the right of way ahead with the stream/ditch to your left for about 1 mile.

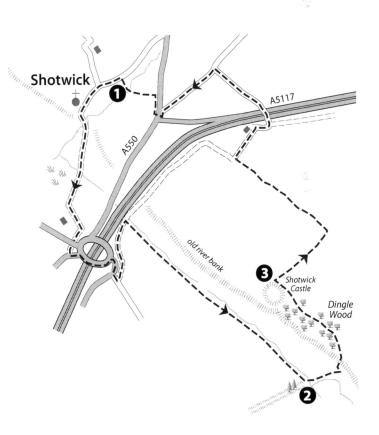

2. After several fields you approach a hedge line ahead with a line of pines. These mark the line of an old seawall; one of several built during the late eighteenth century to reclaim the land around nearby Sealand.

Cross the stile in the corner of the field by the gate and you will see what remains of the seawall to the right. Cross the stile and footbridge on the left in a few yards (passing back into England) and another stile into a field. Walk ahead initially with a ditch on the right, then cut directly across the field to go through a kissing gate onto a farm track. Turn left along the track and immediately before a large field gate, turn right into woods.

The path climbs up a wooded bank, then levels to follow the top of the bank.

This bank is the old coastline of Wirral before the Dee was diverted into the 'New Cut' on the Welsh side of the river, allowing the vast reclamation schemes of the late eighteenth century. The name of nearby Sealand recalls these schemes.

Ignore footpaths on the right keeping ahead to cross a wooden footbridge. The path continues ahead on the obvious path through the woods away from the old riverbank crossing another wooden footbridge.

3. Cross a small brick footbridge and go through a kissing gate to enter fields by the earthworks of Shotwick Castle. Turn right and walk beside the fence with the earthworks and mounds associated with the castle on the left. There is a small information panel in the far corner of the field by a kissing gate.

These mounds, which stand close to the old shoreline, are all that now remain of Shotwick Castle, built to defend the English-Welsh border during the early medieval period. Remnants of the stone walls, which stood until the seventeenth century, have all been removed now and were probably used locally as building materials.

The castle is thought to have been built by Hugh 'Lupus', Earl of Chester and later used by the English Kings in their wars with the Welsh and Irish during the Middle Ages. Henry II led an army against

Wales in 1156 from Wirral and probably retreated to Shotwick eleven years later following his defeat on the Berwyn Mountains. In the following century both Henry III and Edward I passed through Shotwick on their way to conquests in Wales and Ireland and almost certainly stayed at the castle.

By the close of the thirteenth century, the death of Prince Llywelyn and the conquest of Edward I led to peace with the Welsh and the military importance of the castle declined.

Go through the kissing gate by the information panel and walk ahead through two large fields beside the hedge. At the top of the second field turn left through a kissing gate and follow the right of way ahead along the field edge. Cross a footbridge in the field corner and continue ahead through the following fields.

The earthworks of Shotwick Castle and information board

A few yards after crossing a farm track, turn right over a foot-bridge and continue with the hedge on your left. Cross another farm track by two kissing gates and turn right up a surfaced bridleway towards a farm. Pass the farm over on the left and at the end of the bridleway turn right along the tarmac access road. Follow the road as it curves left across the bridge over the dual carriageway. After the bridge follow the lane ahead to the T junction at the end.

Turn left and walk down the lane to the road junction where there is a crossing by traffic lights. It is best to use the crossing here as this is a fast road! Cross the road with care and turn right. In about 100m or so take the signed footpath to 'Shotwick' on the left.

Go through the kissing gate and bear half-right through a field to a small gate in the corner. Go through the gate and a kissing gate in a few yards leads into a sloping field on the left. Descend this field to a footbridge over the stream in the bottom right corner. Cross the footbridge and rise up the field to 'Shotwick Lane' to complete the walk.

Dibbinsdale & Brotherton Park

Distance: 5¾ miles/9.25km

This is a surprising walk passing through a contrasting land-scape of urban and industrial development, as well as quiet woods and riverside paths.

Start: There is a large car park at Eastham Country Park, situated at the end of 'Ferry Road' in Eastham just beyond the 'The Tap' pub.
Grid ref. 365 818 (Landranger 117, Explorer 266).

The walk

1. Leaving the car park, return to the mini roundabout and turn left along a short road which leads to a parking area. At the end of the car park continue ahead on a tarmac footpath which stays close to the river bank. At a road junction, keep ahead to another small car park overlooking the river.

There are wide views across the River Mersey from here to the famous Liverpool skyline with the two cathedrals most prominent.

Follow the cycle path beyond the car park, keeping left at a fork. The cycle way stays close to the river, before eventually swinging left to reach to an industrial estate road. Turn right and follow the road to a T junction. Turn left here following the cycle way which runs along the left-hand side of the road.

Just before the end of the road ('Commercial Road'), cross over and turn right with the cycle way. Cross an access road ('Georgia

Avenue') and immediately after the next access road, cross the bridge ahead (over a disused railway line) following the cycle way as it curves right-wards down to the old track bed. Follow the cycle way under the bridge and through a rock cutting. After a second bridge the cycle way swings right out of the cutting to pass along a raised section above the River Dibbins.

2. After the river, look for a path on the left that leads down to the road. Follow this path and turn sharp left down the road. At the bottom of the hill there is a mini roundabout. Go ahead across the roundabout and the river, then cross the road and go through a gate on the right. This leads into 'Brotherton Park and Dibbinsdale Local Nature Reserve'.

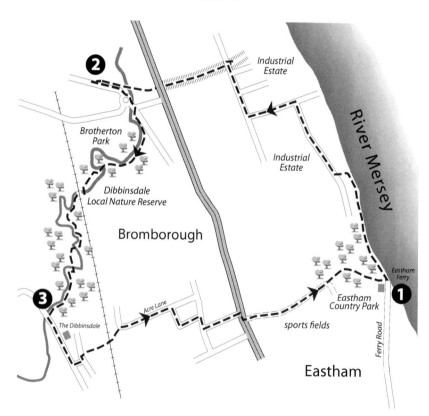

Dibbinsdale woods

If you have not been here before you will likely be surprised by the unspoilt beauty of this little green oasis in such an unlikely setting. The traffic is quickly left behind and the path takes you beneath sandstone cliffs cut by the river and through quiet woods. This is Dibbinsdale, which has managed to survive the relentless tide of development surrounding it.

Keep to the path beside the river (ignoring paths on the left). At a prominent fork keep ahead and a little further on cross the river by a wooden footbridge. In about 50m turn left on a path that swings back towards the river again. Cross a footbridge and pass through a tunnel beneath the Chester to Birkenhead rail line.

Beyond the tunnel, continue on the good footpath through the woods, soon beside the river again. At a junction, follow the main path ahead across two footbridges and bear left through an open meadow. At the far side of the meadow cross the river again by another footbridge. Turn right immediately after the bridge and follow the path through the woods to reach the road.

3. Turn left up the hill passing 'The Dibbinsdale' (pub). Turn left into 'Blyth Road' and at the T junction turn left again. In about 50m, opposite 'Greenacre Drive', cross over and take the signed path to 'Acre Lane' which passes between gardens on the right. After playing fields, cross a road and continue on the path opposite which leads over the railway to join 'Acre Lane'.

Bear right along the road passing shops and the Professional Excellence Centre and turn right into 'Mossley Avenue'. At the end of the road turn left and at the next junction opposite 'Mendell Primary School' turn right. In about 100m turn left into 'Neville Road' and follow this road down to the busy A41. Turn right for about 40m then cross over and follow the signed bridleway (BR 32) to 'Eastham Country Park'.

Follow the bridleway until it turns right into sports fields (Warren Lane). Keep ahead here into Eastham Country Park and follow the main footpath back to the car park to complete the walk.

Mara Books

Mara Books publish a range of walking books for Cheshire and North Wales and have the following list to date. A complete list of current titles is available on our web site:

www.marabooks.co.uk *or* www.northerneyebooks.co.uk

Cheshire
Leisure walks series

Short walks from Wirral villages
ISBN 978-1-902512-23-5. A collection of 30 short walks designed with the less able walker in mind. They are ideal for family groups with young children or the elderly. They seek out level, well-maintained footpaths with distances ranging from just 1 mile to a maximum of 4¾ miles.

Walks in Mysterious Cheshire and Wirral
ISBN 978-0-9553557-0-7. Second edition. A collection of 14 themed circular walks exploring Cheshire's historic landscape.

Walks in West Cheshire and Wirral
ISBN 978-0-9553557-2-1. Thirty of the best walks to be enjoyed in west Cheshire and Wirral.

Circular walks along the Sandstone Trail
ISBN 978-1-902512-10-5. A well established title, now in its fifth edition, featuring 13 linked circular walks ranged along the popular Sandstone Trail.

Walking Cheshire's Sandstone Trail
ISBN 978-1-908632-01-2. The official guide to Cheshire's premier walking route. The trail is described in detail and is illustrated with full colour photographs and Ordnance Survey mapping.

North Wales
Leisure walks series

Coastal Walks around Anglesey
ISBN 978-1-902512-20-4. A collection of circular walks which explore the varied scenery of Anglesey's beautiful coastline.

Walking on the Lleyn Peninsula
ISBN 978-1-902512-00-6. A collection of circular walks exploring the wild and beautiful coastline and hills of the Lleyn Peninsula.

Circular Walks in the Conwy Valley
ISBN 978-0-9522409-7-6. A collection of circular walks which explore the varied scenery of this beautiful valley, from the Great Orme to Betws-y-Coed.

Walking in Northern Snowdonia
ISBN 978-1-902512-06-8. Twenty of the best low-level walks in northern half of the Snowdonia National Park.

Walking in the Clwydian Range
ISBN 978-1-902512-14-3. A collection of 21 circular walks exploring the Clwydian Range Area of Outstanding Natural Beauty (AONB).

Walking in the Vale of Clwyd and Hiraethog
ISBN 978-0-9559625-3-0. A collection of circular walks exploring the Denbigh Moors and the Vale of Clwyd.

Best Walks in North Wales
ISBN 978-0-9553557-3-8. A collection of 28 of the very best circular walks ranged throughout North Wales, from the wilds of the Lleyn Peninsula through Anglesey and Snowdonia to the rolling hills of the Clwydian Range.